Praise for **The Every Day MBA**

'*The Every Day MBA* shows you that what really matters is learning to think, to reflect and to develop yourself as a manager and leader.'

Mike Pedler, Emeritus Professor at Henley Business School, University of Reading

'This is an invaluable guide for any manager looking to apply MBA thinking in the real world. The importance of taking time to reflect is often forgotten; this book reinforces the value of thinking deeply about what we do as leaders. Strongly recommended.'

Gordon Seabright, Director of the Eden Project

'Packed with insights, tools, tips, cases and know-how, this easy-to-read book will accelerate your ability to deal with challenging management issues. A must for every manager.'

Jessica Pryce-Jones, Joint CEO, iOpener Institute for People and Performance

'This fantastic book helps you to challenge the mental barriers of the status quo and to achieve real improvements.'

Peter Meier, CEO, Kuoni Travel Holding Ltd

The Every Day MBA

The Every Day MBA

How to turn world-class business thinking into everyday business brilliance

Chris Dalton, PhD

PEARSON

Harlow, England • London • New York • Boston • San Francisco • Toronto • Sydney
Auckland • Singapore • Hong Kong • Tokyo • Seoul • Taipei • New Delhi
Cape Town • São Paulo • Mexico City • Madrid • Amsterdam • Munich • Paris • Milan

Pearson Education Limited
Edinburgh Gate
Harlow CM20 2JE
United Kingdom
Tel: +44 (0)1279 623623
Web: www.pearson.com/uk

First published 2015 (print and electronic)

Pearson Education is not responsible for the content of third-party internet sites.

ISBN: 978-1-292-01674-0 (print)
       978-1-292-01676-4 (PDF)
       978-1-292-01677-1 (ePub)
       978-1-292-01675-7 (eText)

British Library Cataloguing-in-Publication Data
A catalogue record for the print edition is available from the British Library

Library of Congress Cataloging-in-Publication Data
Dalton, Chris.
  The every day MBA / Chris Dalton, PhD.
    pages cm
  Includes index.
  ISBN 978-1-292-01674-0 (limp) -- ISBN 978-1-292-01676-4 (PDF) -- ISBN
978-1-292-01677-1 (ePub) -- ISBN 978-1-292-01675-7 (eText)
  1. Management. 2. Strategic planning. 3. Master of business administration
degree. I. Title.
  HD31.D197 2015
  658--dc23
                        2014036235

10 9 8 7 6 5 4 3 2 1
18 17 16 15 14

Cover design by Rob Day

Print edition typeset in Melior Com 7.5pt by 3
Print edition printed in Great Britain by Henry Ling Ltd, at the Dorset Press,
Dorchester, Dorset

NOTE THAT ANY PAGE CROSS REFERENCES REFER TO THE PRINT EDITION

For Amy and Zsófi

Contents

List of figures

Acknowledgements

The scope of subject matter of *The Every Day MBA* contains one real limitation for a book, namely there will always be more ideas than pages available. Some themes are absent; for example, entrepreneurship, family-run businesses, managerial research methods, changing patterns of work and career, these may be essential for future editions. Not everything can fit, but perhaps not everything should. Business school students nowadays need courses in statistics or computing, and some topics, such as business law, may be too specific to do justice to here. What remains is a good oversight of the essentials of MBA practice and thinking.

I want to show my sincere appreciation for the support I have received from many individuals while writing *The Every Day MBA*. I must thank all the past and present MBA students who have given me on-going feedback on drafts, in particular Rupa Datta and Nora Egger. My faculty colleagues at Henley Business School have been invaluable, but I'll single out Carole Print, Chris Worthington and Peter Race. My editor and patient guide through this process at Pearson, Chris Cudmore, and at home my patient wife, Gina, both deserve medals.

Publisher's acknowlegements

We are grateful to the following for permission to reproduce copyright material:

Figures

Figure 2.1 adapted from *Identity and the Life Cycle* (Erikson, E. 1994), W.W. Norton & Co. Ltd; Figure 3.3 from *Competitive Advantage* (Porter, M.E. 2004), Simon & Schuster, with the permission of The Free Press, a Division of Simon & Schuster, Inc., all rights reserved; Figure 4.1 from *In Search of Excellence* (Peters, T.J. and Waterman, R.H. 1982), McKinsey & Company; Figure 4.2 adapted from *Psychological Contracts in Organizations: Understanding written and unwritten agreements* (Rousseau, D.M. 1995), Sage Publications, Inc.; Figure 4.3 adapted from 'Developmental sequence in small groups', *Psychological Bulletin*, 63(6): 384-99 (Tuckman, B. 1965), American Psychological Association; Figure 4.4 from a report by Purcell, J., Kinnie, N., Hutchinson, S., Rayton, B. and Swart, J. (2003) 'Understanding the People and Performance Link: Unlocking the Black Box', with the permission of the Chartered Institute of Personnel and Development. London (**www.cipd.co.uk**); Figure 6.1 from 'A stakeholder approach to relationship marketing strategy: The development and use of the "six markets" model', *European Journal of Marketing*, 39(7/8): 855-871 (Payne, A., Ballantyne, D. and Christopher, M. 2005), Emerald Group Publishing Ltd; Figure 7.1 from McKinsey & Company in collaboration with General Electric; Figure 9.2 from *The Competitive Advantage of Nations* (Porter, M.E. 1990), Simon & Schuster, with the permission of The Free Press, a Division of Simon & Schuster, Inc., all rights reserved; Figure 10.1 adapted from *The Managerial Grid III: The key to leadership excellence* (Blake, R. and Mouton, J. 1985), Gulf Publishing Company; Figure 10.2 adapted from *Action-Centred Leadership* (Adair, J.E. 1973), McGraw-Hill Education; Figure 10.4 from **http://www. kotterinternational.com/our-principles/changesteps/changesteps**, Kotter International; Figure 11.1 from 'Toward a theory of stakeholder identification and salience: Defining the principle of who and what really counts', *The Academy* *of Management Review*, 22(4): 853-886 (Mitchell, R., Agle, B. and Wood, D. 1997), The Academy of Management; Figure 11.2 adapted from 'The pyramid of corporate social responsibility: Toward the moral management of organizational stakeholders', *Business Horizons*, 34(4): 39-48 (Carroll, A.B. 1991), Elsevier.

Text

Quote on page 33 from http://www.ted.com/talks/ bill_and_melinda_gates_why_giving_away_our_wealth_has_been_ the_most_satisfying_thing_we_ve_done, TED Conferences LLC; Quote on page 34 from www.gatesfoundation.org, Bill and Melinda Gates Foundation; Extract on page 73, including a quote from Don McLaughlin, vice president of employee experience at Cisco, from a February 2014 article in *Talent Magazine*, www.talentmgt.com/articles/divide-and-conquer, Copyright © 1995–2014 MediaTec Publishing Inc and Cisco Systems, Inc.; Extract on page 128 from http://www.ab-inbev. com/go/media/annual_report_2013, Anheuser-Busch InBev; Extract on page 129 from http://www.ab-inbev.com/go/brands/ brand_strategy, Anheuser-Busch InBev; Extract on page 141 from http://www.pg.com/en_US/company/purpose_people/pvp. shtml, The Procter & Gamble Company; Extract on page 145 from 'Trader Media drives from print to digital', *The Financial Times*, 19/02/2013 (Budden, R.), © The Financial Times Limited. All Rights Reserved; Extract on page 161 from 'WEEK IN REVIEW – PHARMACEUTICALS – Pfizer walks away from controversial Astra offer', *The Financial Times*, 31/05/2014 (Wilson, N.), © The Financial Times Limited. All Rights Reserved; Extract on page 231 from http://www.intel.co.uk/content/dam/doc/policy/policy-conflict-minerals.pdf, Intel Corporation; Quote on page 236 from Nicky Chambers of Best Foot Forward (UK).

In some instances we have been unable to trace the owners of copyright material, and we would appreciate any information that would enable us to do so.

About the author

I have more than 22 years of experience in management education and training. I work at Henley Business School, at the University of Reading in the UK, where I am Associate Professor of Management Learning. My specialist area is Personal Development and I teach MBA workshops, run corporate workshops and lead seminars related to management development in many parts of the world. In the past I have been Director for the Henley Distance Learning (Flexible) MBA, a programme with more than 3,000 executives worldwide, and Director of the full-time and modular MBA programmes at the Central European University Business School in Budapest, Hungary. I'm passionate about the power of reflection in management education. I hold a PhD in Management Learning and Leadership from Lancaster University and an MBA from Henley.

Networking is an important skill for MBAs, so you're welcome to sign up to my blog at **www.chris-dalton.com**, follow me on Twitter @dalty, or start engaging with fellow readers in the open-access LinkedIn group for *The Every Day MBA* at **https://www.linkedin.com/groups/ Every-Day-MBA-7420755/about**. I'm always interested in hearing your views, suggestions or experience at chris.dalton@henley.ac.uk.

About this book

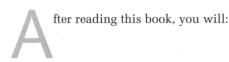fter reading this book, you will:

✓ understand key concepts, theories and models of an MBA

✓ be ready to apply new ways of thinking to your job

✓ be able to hold informed conversations with colleagues with MBAs

✓ reflect on, re-evaluate and improve your performance

✓ realise that you knew more than you thought, and ...

✓ begin to appreciate how much more there is to know! Learning is a life-long process.

This book is for:

▌ aspiring/new managers and managers with great experience but no MBA

▌ anyone interested in accelerating their career in business or management

▌ managers who already have an MBA but want to refresh or continue their development

▌ learning and development leaders in any organisation that values MBA thinking and behaviours

▌ educators and trainers who want to understand how MBAs think.

Introduction

Welcome to *The Every Day MBA*. This book is a guide to applying world-class MBA principles and thinking at work.

Whether you have ambitions to do an MBA or already have one, in business and management those three letters certainly seem to exert quite a hold over the imagination. Every year, tens of thousands of managers around the world invest their time, energy and money to graduate with a master's degree in business administration. No book can equal that achievement or capture everything that years of study contain. It can, however, highlight two things that graduates from top business schools have discovered:

1. The most lasting benefit of an MBA is a change in your thinking.
2. Informed self-awareness is the key to new behaviours, better decision making and continuing career growth.

Presumably managers already think, otherwise their actions would just be automatic. So what is so special about the change in thinking brought about by an MBA? One answer could be simply that MBA thinking accelerates promotion to the next level. True, but a more powerful idea is that the best MBAs are people educated to see a special relationship between thinking and action that can make a real difference to achievement at work, one's career, and the impact of business on a changing world. So, using clear and concise language, this book will use the typical structure and experience of an MBA to challenge you to apply ideas and new ways of thinking about what you do.

Key points about this book

Each chapter covers a crucial area of management and leadership featured in MBA study. You will find overviews of concepts, key models, frameworks and theories, as well as real-world illustrations. You will be encouraged to practise the types of thinking developed in the top programmes around the world.

Three assumptions underpin *The Every Day MBA* and I want you to keep them in mind as you work through the book.

1 An MBA links practice and theory

Academic rigour mixed with practical, industry-specific knowledge of the kind that you develop simply by doing your job is a powerful equation. MBAs are good at combining these different kinds of knowledge. True, the more experience of the workplace you have, the more you can get from this book, but if you are at an early point in your career, you will find many ways to apply MBA thinking to the lessons that the first few years of management always bring.

2 An MBA challenges deep-set habits

What is required and rewarded early in a management career is not necessarily what is required or suitable at more senior levels. Success at entry and middle levels needs certain skills, but some of these habits can become barriers later in your career. Many of our habits are deep-set and are often taken for granted. They are difficult to spot and even harder to change or let go. An MBA is all about such personal development.

3 An MBA addresses what it really takes to become a senior manager or leader

Business is now a global phenomenon. In only the last 50 years the world has changed beyond recognition and no doubt it will be transformed again completely in the coming half century. Business schools are no better or worse at predicting the future than the rest of society, but they are great places to develop the critical and reflective thinking abilities required to work in uncertainty and change. It is not about what you learn, it is about knowing how you learn, how you think and how you act as a leader. With awareness and dedication, you can begin to prepare yourself for leadership roles now.

Structure of the book

The Every Day MBA is organised in four parts.

Part 1 (Chapters 1–2) is about management, MBAs and you, and how to apply this book. Like many at the start of an actual MBA you may be tempted to skip the first section and jump to the 'real stuff' in Part 2. Try to resist this because self-awareness and good preparation are key to learning. Before you start to read about the various parts of management practice, you need to invest some time becoming aware of yourself and your experience. Personal development is knowing how to reflect on practice so that you can see immediate results as well as preparing for the future.

Part 2 (Chapters 3–5) is about tactical thinking in management. We examine the core subject areas of the first phase of an MBA, highlighting commonly used models and insightful theories. Each part links to one of the types of thinking used by an MBA, and you will be able to follow suggestions to apply these to your management practice.

Part 3 (Chapters 6–9) moves on to strategic thinking and concerns the internal and external environment of organisations. This part of the MBA brings to the fore the idea of managing relationships, including the ones an organisation has with its customers and its competitors, as well as the complex task of understanding the rapidly changing nature of international business.

Part 4 (Chapters 10–12) looks at critical thinking in leadership and management. This might be the most challenging part of the book because it deals with visionary thinking in management. By visionary I mean the special kind of future-focused pattern recognition that flows from tactical and strategic thinking. Personal development means stretching your horizons and testing your assumptions as a manager, so the final chapter offers some advice for self-awareness and meeting the challenges of management and career.

Look out for plenty of suggestions for **activities for reflective practice** throughout the book. Again, you may be tempted to skip these, but they are essential because such tasks get you exploring what you and others do in your organisation. They may well challenge some of your core assumptions. In addition, at the end of each chapter there are suggestions for further reading and extra questions that will help your personal development.

A **glossary** containing management and MBA thinking concepts appears at the end. In the text, glossary entries are *bold italics* when they first appear.

How to make *The Every Day MBA* work for you

Reflection n. [rɪˈflɛkʃ(ə)n]: serious thought and consideration

Management is a practical activity and the key to being a better manager lies in thoughtful action. The reality you encounter every day can be your teacher only if you are awake to it. The majority of managers, however, are not awake. Their training has prepared them neither to notice nor to think for themselves. Organisations put their money and faith in training to correct this, but with only limited success. What about education? There are thousands of business schools, but believe it or not, there is no hard evidence to show that the MBA curriculum makes for better decision making. Good business schools are amazing places, but what these schools know is that while content is important, education is about creating the right conditions to develop managerial identity and purpose.

Here are six things you can do to promote the right conditions and attitude for reading *The Every Day MBA*:

1. Keep a notebook with you at all times (without lines, if possible, to get you out of the habit of thinking in lists). Have plenty of pens and pencils to write with. Write things down.

2. Our brains work through association, so start connecting to new ideas using the same principles your mind functions with. Learn how to draw a mind map (visit Tony Buzan's website **www.thinkbuzan.com** if you are not already familiar with this fantastic tool).

3. *Consciously* decide to become curious. Be an explorer. Curiosity is essential to creativity. Catch yourself whenever you say 'Yes, *but* ...' and replace that with 'Yes, *and* ...' and see the difference it makes.

4. Rate yourself for each of the following and indicate whether you think you are below, at or above average.[1]

	I'm below average	I'm average	I'm above average
My IQ			
My skill as a manager			
My skill as a leader			
My analytical skills			
My critical thinking skills			
My self-awareness			
My interpersonal skills			
My creativity			

5 Write down the three most important words or phrases in your life. Ask a significant person in your life to do the same. Discuss the result. What do you value most?

6 Watch the TED talk given by Sir Ken Robinson in 2013 entitled 'How to escape education's Death Valley' and reflect on the message about intelligence, creativity and education.[2] Create a mind map of your thoughts.

Now you're ready.

Notes

1 Research shows that potential employers are mostly looking for the last four, not the first four.

2 www.ted.com/talks/ken_robinson_how_to_escape_education_s_death_valley.html

Management and the MBA

The great myth is the manager as orchestra conductor. It's this idea of standing on a pedestal and you wave your baton and accounting comes in, and you wave it somewhere else and marketing chimes in with accounting, and they all sound very glorious. But management is more like orchestra conducting during rehearsals, when everything is going wrong.

Henry Mintzberg, quoted in the *Wall Street Journal*, 2009[1]

In a nutshell

The need for skilled managers has never been greater, and globally the number of people in management is set to grow in the coming decades. The MBA reigns supreme as the badge of quality in business administration, yet only 1 in every 200 managers will get to do one. A business degree is a great thing, but you don't need one to start thinking about purpose and contribution to the bottom line. With discipline and curiosity you can make huge strides in your professional life.

In this chapter you will:

▌ learn about the history and main functions of management

▌ define the purpose of management

▌ discover the structure and goals of the MBA

▌ write your first reflections and do your first activities for reflective practice

Why this book?

There may be many reasons why you have decided to read this book. Perhaps you are new to management and are feeling a bit overwhelmed. Equally, you could have plenty of experience but feel stuck in your career, as though you have reached a plateau. You may have a long list of specialist qualifications under your belt and are now beginning to think about an MBA as the next step. Or maybe you don't have formal education behind you, have improvised from day one and somehow fear being exposed for this (by the way, this is known as the 'imposter syndrome' and is a lot more common in management than you might think). Alternatively, you may just be curious about business and education in general, or incredibly busy and feel that if you were better informed you would have a little more control over your career path.

Whatever your story, there will be something in *The Every Day MBA* from which you can benefit. But to find it you will need to do some critical thinking and some reflective writing as you go. So before anything else here are your first tasks.

QUESTIONS FOR REFLECTION

1 Why did you pick up this book?

2 What is your management style? How would a colleague describe you?

As you go through *The Every Day MBA*, I want you to develop the habit of regularly making such notes – this is one of the things that will lead you to reflective practice (more on this in Chapter 2) and in Parts 2, 3 and 4 you will find a couple of reflection questions at the end of each chapter.

An open mindset is the only route to insights from this book. Critical practice – that is, doing it with your eyes wide open – is a key facet of an MBA, so you will also see regular suggestions for things to apply or ideas to investigate in your own job. Here is the first.

ACTIVITIES FOR REFLECTIVE PRACTICE

1. Make a list of at least three assumptions you make about management. State the obvious. The more basic, the better.

2. Now think about your organisation. List another three things you take for granted or never question about the place where you work. Look for things that 'need no explanation'. Discuss your lists with friends or work colleagues.

Assumption naming is an important thinking skill, but not an easy one. Even if you rated yourself as 'above average' in critical thinking skills in the list I gave earlier, you may struggle to name all your own assumptions in your day-to-day activities as a manager. Carrying out these reflective tasks is part of training yourself to challenge how you see the world.

Management

Since this is a book about management and the MBA we should start by understanding what these terms mean.

Having a job is nothing new, but the role of management is a relatively modern notion. It has roots in the industrial revolution more than 200 years ago, so its meaning was forged in an era of corporate invention, mass production, division of labour and admiration for the methods of science. Industrialised societies have benefited from unparalleled advances in technology, improvements in public health and social welfare, establishment of global trade, and high standards of education. Yet they have also seen exponential growth in human population, unquestioning exploitation of natural resources, destructive armed conflicts at every level from local to global, and repeated cycles of economic boom and bust. For better and worse, there can be little doubt that today business shapes our world.

> there can be little doubt that today business shapes our world

There has never been a shortage of thinkers to make sense of all of this. In 1916 French mining engineer Henri Fayol published a **seminal** text on management.[2] It contained six functions of management that have proved quite resilient:

1. Forecasting and planning.

2. Organising.

3. Commanding or directing.

4. Coordinating.

5. Developing outputs.

6. Controlling (through feedback).

Fayol's views were echoed by others. For example, American engineer Frederick W. Taylor championed management as a precise science of time and motion. 'Taylorism' belongs to a classical view of management built around **technical** *rationality*, and though it may now seem outdated, many organisations still owe something to it. The Ford Motor Company applied it to assembly-line production and Total Quality Management (TQM) united, for a time, organisational hierarchy and supply chain in every department, as Six Sigma attempts to do today.

The most influential voice shaping our understanding of the organisation of business in the second half of the twentieth century was Peter Drucker, who wrote extensively on the role of management in a wide variety of settings. Drucker made a number of accurate predictions and coined many terms, such as 'knowledge worker', 'outsourcing' and 'management by objective'. One of the reasons his work remains important today is his consistent belief that management is a matter of hierarchy and relationship.

Do these views still hold true today? Well, yes, and no.

Yes, in that we often rely on the past to show us the way to the future. Organisations, like people, derive a sense of identity from what has gone before and there are many turning points from the past that, for better or worse, still matter in management thinking. Consider just three:

- In 1888, a US court held that a private corporation was entitled to the same constitutional protection in law as a US citizen, and the concept of 'corporate personhood' was born. The results? First, a population explosion of businesses that are born (and die) every year around the world. Second, we are now comfortable thinking of organisations as if they have minds, identities, rights and ambitions entirely of their own. Third, huge diversity in what these corporate persons do, but almost no disparity in how they are organised (that is, they all tend to have the same basic structure).

- From 1927 to 1932 Elton Mayo conducted a series of experiments at Western Electric's Hawthorne plant in

Chicago. A good management scientist, his original aim had been research on how the company's lighting products could boost productivity on any manufacturing shop-floor. What he unintentionally found was that productivity under experimental conditions increased no matter what variable was changed. At the time, no one made the connection with the experimental context itself. Less significance was seen in the social aspect of the study until the 1950s when, in a new era of behavioural psychology, others revisited these results and concluded that productivity had improved because supervisors and staff paid attention to each other. The 'Hawthorne effect' was coined and the **human relations movement** was born.

In the late 1950s the Gordon and Howell report (in the UK)[3] and the Ford and Carnegie Foundation report (in the US)[4] strongly advocated the use of principles and practices from management science in the education of managers at business schools. Universities invested heavily in their business schools, the management disciplines took shape and the MBA took off.

This legacy still influences how your organisation is set up and these and other landmark moments have shaped management. But they are not the whole story. Management is constantly shifting and its definition is broad. Like all science, it will continue to evolve, but there is still no single, over-arching 'theory' of management.

When economic times are hard, management is often blamed. Many (including some insiders) have accused business schools of being part of the problem, not the solution. Renowned Indian academic Sumantra Ghoshal warned against MBAs relying too much on the 'gloomy' economic theory of greed and self-interest dominating business.[5] Ghoshal believed that the job of senior management was not to change people but to change the context so that those people could flourish. Canadian strategy guru Henry Mintzberg has appealed to MBAs to use more thoughtful reflection on experience in the classroom.[6] After the global economic downturn in 2008, many MBA programmes have been trying to learn these lessons themselves. There are indeed many issues in today's business environment that call for new thinking, such as the following:

▌ An increasing number of people see the (post) industrial business world as a system in runaway, a vicious cycle unsustainable not just in the long run but in the medium term, too. According to this view, the same thinking that created this situation cannot be used to find a solution, and the challenge is one of finding a sustainable model for business using a different way of thinking.

▌ Knowledge has long been a currency of global business, but data is now so freely and quickly available that our definitions of knowledge, and of information, will need to change to reflect this. Knowledge is no longer power. This may seem an odd thing to say in education, and about an MBA, because there are still plenty of items of knowledge crammed into the course, but power now comes from how you share information.

▌ The key to managing or leading others is no longer authority and positions of power in a hierarchy but rather your self-awareness and skills in connecting all the resources around you.

ACTIVITIES FOR REFLECTIVE PRACTICE

1 What do you think the role of management in business is?

2 How is management defined in the organisation you work for?

The purpose of management: value creation

Management is a proxy activity. It becomes necessary to have someone stand in for founders or shareholders when an organisation becomes too big for those people to run it on their own. Therefore, fundamentally a manager represents the interests of others; they cannot do entirely what they please. Another word for this interest is value. Management must create value, and wherever you are in an organisation you need to understand what is meant by this.

> another word for this interest is value

Value is traditionally measured in business by money (e.g. by economic profit, which we cover in Chapter 5), but it can and should also be measured in other ways. Although profit margin is one measure, there are other metrics that can measure value, such as a care for what your customers are getting from the relationship, how suppliers are in tune with your internal processes or the extent to which your fellow employees are contributing to those processes.

When it comes down to it, the world wants managers who can:

- make decisions under uncertainty
- gather, process and analyse information quickly and thoroughly
- communicate effectively on paper and face to face
- see the strategic connection inherent in every situation.

To get all these things done, especially in larger organisations, the role of management is often divided into three levels: first, middle and senior.

First-level managers have three main tasks to take care of:

▍ **Learning from doing**: gaining hands-on experience of the subject matter in their part of the organisation is the best way to pick up basic knowledge skills. Another way of saying this is on-the-job training.

▍ **Learning the ropes**: behind all the processes and systems lies the culture of the organisation – this is the 'how we do things round here' part, and is how it actually works.

▍ **Taking on responsibility and decision making** to complete relatively basic management tasks such as meeting agreed targets or mastering limited staff supervision and development.

The politics of the organisation are rarely an obstacle at this level because there is little that you can do (usually ...) to rock the boat.

Middle managers have all these – plus three more:

▍ **An informed curiosity**: a hunger for new knowledge and for new ways of doing the job better.

▍ **Self-preservation**: the practical necessity to align with senior management's definition of value creation. This is a big one. Managers are constrained in what they can and can't do and must weigh up day-to-day decision making between what subject knowledge and experience tell them and what politics will allow or condone.

▍ **Responsibility for implementing small- to medium-scale change**: middle management. This is mostly a process of adjusting what is already there, as opposed to creating things from scratch. Middle managers rarely get the chance for visionary leadership.

Effective middle managers may be given the chance eventually to lead at the top. Then, as senior managers they get to do all the things above, plus three additional tasks:

▍**Stand in place of the founder or owners**: their task is, above all else, to decide what will maximise rather than destroy value for the shareholders of a business. This is despite the owners being only one category of stakeholder, and value being measurable in many other ways.

▍**Translate the vision and set the strategy**: ultimately they are responsible not just for the direction but also for the consequences of everybody's actions.

▍**Keep eyes and ears open**: continuously survey and interact with the external environment and prepare for the future context.

Truly successful organisations are those that create an environment of possibility, trust and openness, where middle managers can reach their full potential as they create value for stakeholders. That, however, is rarely the case. Few people work harder than middle managers because they are the bridge between day-to-day operational tasks and the big picture, but in organisations with a confused context at the senior management level, their efforts can end in frustration and burn-out.

The good news is that the MBA is very relevant to the tasks of middle management and as preparation for the complexities and challenges of senior management and leadership. This is exciting. With the right ingredients, MBA thinking can be life-changing.

QUESTIONS FOR REFLECTION

1 Which level of management do you work in? What tells you this?

2 How do you feel within this organisation? Make some notes under the following headings: long-term commitment, material rewards, current emotional state, professional pride.

In summary, management involves:

▌ acting with thoughtful purpose and intention

▌ being the symbolic but active representative of the owners of a business or organisation

▌ consciously using resources to create value in a way that is socially and ethically acceptable

▌ setting the context for future performance.

The MBA

We've discussed what management is, now we'll look in a bit more detail at the MBA degree.

The MBA is a generalist degree. It was first offered at Harvard in 1908, but management remained stubbornly vocational for several decades after that. In fact, the MBA did not gain much acceptance until the 1950s when shifts in education policy and economic growth following the Second World War combined to create demand for qualified practitioners. It has not looked back. In the United States alone more than 250,000 people are currently studying for an MBA, offered to them by nearly 1,000 institutions. The MBA now accounts for nearly two-thirds of all graduate business degrees. If you want to do an MBA in the United States, there are plenty of schools to choose from, but expect a two-year full-time course, and an average age among your fellow (largely non-US) classmates of 28.

In Europe, where the MBA arrived in 1957 at INSEAD in France and in 1964 at London Business School, the market is dominated by part-time study and the average age is a lot higher. In emerging economies the degree is rapidly growing as a mass-market product by big business schools in large universities. Class sizes in full-time MBAs may vary from a handful to several hundred, depending on the school. MBAs are expensive. Fees on many MBAs are high and usually don't include living costs or the opportunity cost of a year or two away from employment. Nearly everywhere, men still outnumber women in most MBA classes, as they do in the boardroom – something that business schools ought to be changing.

The stereotype of an MBA is an ambitious, power-hungry and brash male manager investing in a year or two off work, eager to show their competitive zeal and mental agility, and equally eager to trample over their colleagues to finish top of the class and get hired by a leading consultant or bank. There may be some people like that, but actually it's not representative of the majority of students, who are professionals with management experience and fewer expectations that the return on their study will be measured only in salary and bonuses.

Why does anyone do an MBA?

Management is a process of both personal identity and analytical sense making. An MBA involves a lot of work in what is already the busiest period of a person's working life. Reading, writing assignments and exams, classroom discussions and group work, myriad adjustments in work–life balance and major changes in perspective and beliefs – all are typical of the experience. An MBA is about understanding and then managing changes in the web of relationships between senior and middle levels of management. The value of doing one comes from the applicability of what you have learned to a range of industries, in a host of situations, across a world of cultural divides. An MBA will not make you a genius in every field, but it ought to equip you to manage, lead and inspire others who are experts in theirs. This requires good character, astute self-awareness and strong thinking skills.

> an MBA is about understanding and
> then managing changes

So why doesn't everyone do one? The majority of managers in the world will never do an MBA, and not just because there are many more managers than spaces. It's expensive, it consumes time that most people never seem to have in the first place, and it imbalances further the precarious equilibrium of work, family, relationships and other parts of your life. On top of that, there is nothing magic about a business school other than creating the right context for personal development. However, with determination and support you can achieve many of the same results through self-awareness and application to self-study.

MBA thinking: why is it so important?

As we saw in the introduction, this book is about MBA thinking, or thinking like an MBA every day. So let's be clear and precise about thinking, because how you think is part of creating value.

We use the word 'thinking' in a number of ways. It can mean the 'stream' of conscious and semi-conscious images and ideas that passes through our minds, usually unchallenged, every day, or things that are real but not present, except in our imaginations. Equally, it can mean the deliberate mental process linking enquiry/explanation to reasoning/action. It is the last one of these that is MBA thinking. As you read on, keep in mind two important facts about thinking:

1 Thinking is always categorical. In other words, thinking is a way of dividing up a 'messy' world so that we can examine, understand and apply actions to it. As a

manager, if the way you think does not match the way the world is, you will end up in trouble.

2 We all have the ability to think about thinking. This is a skill we can develop.

What are concepts, frameworks, models and theories?

People who do an MBA often get a boost to self-confidence early on. All the new vocabulary and the new concepts you pick up on the course, as well as the quick feedback at work if you are studying part-time, can make a difference to how you feel and how others see you. When you learn about new things, you tend to start to see them around you. This new MBA vocabulary has its own grammar, so it will help to differentiate between a few important terms now:

Concepts: Our way of imposing order on a complex world by defining things – in this case ideas and concepts. When we name, we create categories, so a concept is a way to build a map. Business contains a great number of concepts (e.g. profit, competitive advantage, culture, etc.) and these form the vocabulary of management.

Frameworks: Representations, often visual, of concepts that have something in common. A good framework is useful because it organises your thinking in a structured way. Which way round you order those concepts is not so important.

Models: Collections of concepts arranged a particular way to map the relationships between concepts (e.g. cause and effect), and more detailed than frameworks. Unlike frameworks, with models it matters in which order concepts are placed. Models are short cuts. MBAs, academics and business practitioners like them because they quickly let you apply other people's thinking to a given problem or question.

The statistician George Box once said, 'Essentially, all models are wrong, but some are useful', so keep this in mind.[7]

Theories: Our current best explanations for how we think the world works. Good theories aim to explain as wide a set of phenomena as possible and provide a basis for testing predictions. A better theory is one that explains more than its predecessor. Theories are there to help make sense of incoming information, and are fine-tuned by trying to find their limits. MBAs are not attracted to theory usually until it's too late! Theory building is driven by curiosity.

> when you learn about new things, you tend to start to see them around you

The three phases of a typical MBA programme

Imagine you were creating an MBA curriculum, where would you begin? With strategy? Leadership? Personal development? Study skills? Team building? Or would you launch into one of the functional modules? All these approaches exist, but sooner or later programmes conform to three conventions:

1. Categorising business and management into subjects.
2. Organising those subjects into parts/stages.
3. Sequencing of subjects, usually from simple to complex, functional to strategic and core to elective.

This feels linear, and it is. You might also feel that this does not map exactly onto the messy world as you experience it at work, and it doesn't. But it is a way to organise a lot of ideas and content while you develop your reflective thinking skills as a manager. I want to make *The Every Day MBA* useful for those at work and those studying, so the book will follow the same pattern.

The thinking skills that the MBA develops can be seen to have three phases:

Phase 1 – Tactical: Using facts gained from experience to help make managerial decisions, taking action in line with existing strategy, networking, looking for incremental improvements, 'problem solving'.

Phase 2 – Strategic: Using context, developing a relational view of situations, participating in strategy formation, communicating and implementing strategy, 'problem setting'.

Phase 3 – Critical: Independent learning, systematic questioning of assumptions, mastery, asking unsettling questions, becoming an effective leader, 'problem dissolving'.

Running alongside these is a fourth type of thinking: reflective. It is arguably the most vital, but also the one that many MBA students – and MBA programmes – neglect.

ACTIVITIES FOR REFLECTIVE PRACTICE

1. Talk to at least one person who is in a senior role in your organisation. How did they get into management?
2. Generally, what type of thinking (tactical, strategic or critical) does your current job require from you?

For most people, the career journey is experienced as parts that add up, step by step, to a whole. To be given greater responsibility in management first means proving you are competent at making decisions, solving problems and directing the work of others. Yet in important ways things do change when you become responsible for more. Your decisions are bigger, fewer in number, based on a broader range of considerations and much less reversible.

Putting it together: a blueprint for personal development

At the end of each chapter I will encourage you to think about how each part of the book fits into the bigger picture.

Often we say that we know what a manager is by combining what a manager does with what a manager thinks and knows. Everything you do as a manager happens in relation to everything else and management is by its nature always interconnected. Each chapter in *The Every Day MBA* is a new perspective on the same thing. Before we consider those separate points of view, I want you to consider how much you know about the person you are.

Further reading

A classic text:

HBR's 10 Must Reads: The essentials (2011), Harvard Business Review Press. A collection of seminal articles in *HBR* by the 'big guns' of management thinking.

Going deeper:

A Very Short, Fairly Interesting and Reasonably Cheap Book About Studying Organizations by Chris Grey (2012), Sage Books. I really recommend this book, though it is a challenging read in some parts.

The Corporation: The pathological pursuit of profit and power by Joel Bakan (2005), Robinson Publishing. A timely look into the growth and dominance of our modern business system.

Watch this: 'The transformative power of
                         classical music', classical musician
                         and orchestra conductor Benjamin
                         Zander's powerful TED talk
                         from 2008: **www.ted.com/talks/**
                         benjamin_zander_on_music_and_passion

Notes

1 http://online.wsj.com/news/articles/SB1000142405297020490860457433445O1
79298822
2 Fayol, H. and Storrs, C. (2013) *General and Industrial Management*, Martino
Fine Books.
3 Gordon, R.A. and Howell, J.E. (1959) *Higher Education for Business*,
Columbia University Press.
4 Canning, R.J., Robert, I.D. *et al.* (1961) 'Report of the Committee on the
Study of the Ford and Carnegie Foundation Reports', *Accounting Review*,
American Accounting Association, 191.
5 Ghoshal, S. (2005) 'Bad management theories are destroying good
management practices', *Academy of Management Learning & Education*, 4(1):
75–91.
6 Mintzberg, H. (2004) *Managers, Not MBAs: A hard look at the soft practice
of managing and management development*, Berrett-Koehler Publishers.
7 Box, G. and Draper, N. (1987) *Empirical Model Building and Response
Surfaces*, John Wiley & Sons.

You and your personal development

What lies behind us and what lies before us are tiny matters compared to what lies within.

Ralph Waldo Emerson

In a nutshell

Good MBA programmes rely on students who are both bright and self-aware and I have the same philosophy for this book. I will ask you to reflect on your work and life experience and be honest about what you know and what you don't know (including what you pretend not to know) about yourself. This is part of personal development but it is also linked to having management impact in an organisation.

In this chapter you will:

▌ define reflection and reflective practice

▌ think about different aspects of your personality

▌ look at your strengths and focus on setting development goals

▌ begin to think about your purpose

The keys to personal development

This chapter is unashamedly about you. Before you go further, write down your answers to these questions for reflection.

QUESTIONS FOR REFLECTION

1 When was the last time you were able to stop, think and reflect on your career? Thinking and action go together; what did you do next?

2 We don't usually think about what's important in life until we face a crisis or a serious dilemma. Write some notes about:

(a) the high-point in your life so far and

(b) the lowest point.

'Know thyself' is an ancient instruction. It is both a call for introspective honesty and humility, and a means to know where you belong in society. Personal development involves both your internal and external worlds. Self-awareness is the starting point for learning, so being aware of your personal values, beliefs, capabilities and motivations is a route to emotional maturity in your thinking.

When I begin a personal development journey with a group of MBAs, I want them to do four things:

1 Understand the concepts of reflection and reflective practice.

2 Adopt a mindset of curiosity.

3 Use this curiosity to ask questions.

4 Get into the habit of writing things down.

Taken together, these are a route to action. Time is precious. You're busy and may believe you can't afford to stop and think about what you do. I think that's why you can't afford not to.

Reflection

If you are a mid-career manager, you're probably already too busy to think, let alone reflect. Most managers know **reflection**, if they know it at all, as part of a problem-solving process. Something goes wrong; time is spent collectively or alone reviewing what happened in the hope that identifying the cause will improve the process. But this is limited – reflection is much more than that. I'm as enthusiastic about reflection as Ben Zander (in the TED video mentioned at the end of the previous chapter) is about classical music. So before we go on, here are some truths about reflection:

- It is always about 'unfinished business'; the stuff that just won't go away.

- You can't reflect on something if you haven't noticed it. But reflection is about what is absent. This is a bit of a paradox.

- There are many ways to reflect. Not all of them are comfortable.

- The point of reflection is, in the end, to get unstuck. British philosopher Alan Watts once said, 'We are on a journey to where we are', and I think this is what reflection does for us.

Managers use reflection to three ends. The first category is what I would call technical, or working out what went wrong in order to fix it (as, for example, in a 'lessons learned' or project wash-up). The second category, and the most common in management development, is aligned. This is the careful process of looking at what you need to change or do differently in order to align yourself to the overall goals of your organisation. Finally, there is critical, which is much rarer because it involves questioning assumptions behind your goals, and sometimes comes in response to a major change or trauma where your world has been turned upside down. Most of the reflection you are asked to do in this book will be of the aligned type – you are seeking new ways of steering, not rocking, the boat. If you get further than this, then that's a bonus.

Reflective practice

We like to think of management as a highly ordered and predictable professional activity. But if you think about how your normal working day in management actually goes, the chances are that you don't inhabit a Zen-like, unruffled state of expertise. Rather, you live in a world of constant interruption, surprise and frustration.

> you live in a world of constant interruption, surprise and frustration

In his book *The Reflective Practitioner*, American academic Donald Schön noted that professionals who train for years in the neat and ordered world of theory actually do their jobs in the 'swampy lowlands' of everyday experience.[1] Management happens at the intersection of theory and practice, although most managers learn the skill of 'thinking on their feet' before they become experts in theory. Intuition will work for you up to a point, but becoming expert in identifying underlying assumptions (which often includes the power relations and politics of the office) requires something extra. Reflection is the most important way to think through all the wider concerns than simply the problem in hand.

Curiosity and self-awareness

If you want to apply what is in this book, your curiosity first needs to be woken up. Look back at your answer to the first couple of questions for reflection in Chapter 1. Was curiosity one of the reasons you picked up *The Every Day MBA*? Let's get curious now about four areas of personal development that MBAs often think of at the start of a programme:

Personality: Who am I? What is important to me?

Proficiency: What am I good at? What do I need to develop? What are my goals?

Purpose: What is my contribution to the world?

Practice: What action should I take? What's stopping me?

Let's look at each of these in turn.

Personality: Who am I?

'What makes me the way I am?' 'Is my character from nature or nurture?' 'Is my personality fixed, or can it be changed?' I have learned over the years working alongside even mature MBAs that these are difficult questions to ask. In fact, the big one – 'Who am I?' – is never fully answered.

There are literally hundreds of tools, psychometric tests and questionnaires out there to test a host of theories about personality, and I'll list some below. I believe that personality tests can be useful, but they have limits because any test is only as good as the theory behind it. The vast diversity of questionnaires and models is actually based on only a few core theories of character and personality and the majority of tests are uncritical (and sometimes unaware) of the assumptions made by their underlying theory. One of the main ideas in this book is that you need to develop your ability to think critically, something that becomes more important the higher you get in management. For that reason, I think you should try to find as many ways as possible to investigate your personality.

Values, beliefs and psychometric tests

Values address the 'why' in our lives. Established early in our development, they are principles that are basic to identity and ethical action. Management education often treats them as measurable and rationally worked out by individuals, though a more holistic approach says that values are messy, collective and pre-date language. Our personal values are often apparent only in times of stress, trauma or change and much of the time we tend not to think about them. Until a crisis hits, values remain as unspoken and unquestioned assumptions. Yet it is from our values that we develop beliefs.

> our personal values are often apparent only in times of stress

Beliefs address the 'how' and are guides for how we conduct ourselves from day to day. They are the short cuts we use to make choices in behaviours (the 'what' are the behaviours everybody else actually sees). Beliefs are rules, not opinions. In fact, most of our beliefs are habitual and rarely questioned. Beliefs hold us in place and are the bridge between our actions and our values. If you want to change, learn and grow, you will need to identify which beliefs are self-limiting – and replace them.

Psychometrics is the attempt to measure a person's personality or character. For nearly 100 years, individuals and organisations have used a range of psychometric questionnaires to assess personality and it's likely that you have come across several such instruments in your career. They work by converting a statistical analysis of your responses into a best-guess report on attitudes, aptitudes, traits, characteristics or preferences.

One type of psychometric test measures aptitudes, skills or preferences for behaviour. Understanding what you are good at (or not good at) is a starting point for improving your skills. This popular focus on strengths in management learning is part of the positive psychology movement, which says that you should find out what you are good at ... and do more of it. Tom Rath's best-selling book *StrengthsFinder 2.0* is an example of this concept.[2]

Behaviours and attitudes can change, but personality traits are fixed. Not surprisingly, many of the tests for this aspect of personality were developed from the psychoanalytical tradition. They promise better-informed ways of understanding the self in relation to other types. The best known is the Myers–Briggs Type Indicator (MBTI), an American personality test loosely based on the work of Carl Jung. It is widely used to clarify orientation to the world across four dimensions through innate preferences in how you take in and process information. The four sets of preferences result in 16 personality types. MBTI is similar to the Keirsey Temperament Sorter (accessible online for free). The Five Factor Model uses the acronym OCEAN as a way of remembering what are also called the 'Big Five' personality traits: openness, conscientiousness, extraversion, agreeableness and neuroticism. The result is a very broad way of identifying self-reported traits with behaviours. In a similar way, measures of personal values and belief systems, such as Hogan's Motives, Values and Preferences Inventory (MVPI), encourage you to name your value set from a long list.

Any of these may be a good starting place to think about what's important for you, but psychometrics are seductive, so it's worth remembering a couple of caveats so that you avoid the trap of pigeon-holing:

1 They are not magic. When you fill out a questionnaire about yourself, it's likely that it will tell you what you already know.

2 If the theory behind them is not correct, then the results will be of limited practical value for your personal development in the long run.

It's better to use test scores alongside a range of other sources of information, and to discuss your thoughts with colleagues and friends in order to arrive at an informed view of yourself.

Proficiency: What am I good at?

The statistical measurement of mental intelligence was not an issue until the beginning of the twentieth century. Interest in IQ, or intelligence quotient, was fed by society's needs to find ways to assess and grade children in education and adults in work. Our love of educational testing has not diminished. In recent years the popularity of Daniel Goleman's work on *emotional intelligence* (EI) has also become popular. EI broadly covers self and social awareness, self-management and interpersonal skills and was inspired by Howard Gardner's theory of multiple intelligences. EI is now becoming mainstream for many in learning, and is often combined with growing interest in the neuroscience of learning. Advances in our understanding of what the brain does when we learn have enabled us to map some of the process involved, though this is not quite the same as explaining the meaning of personality.

Nevertheless, 'What am I good at?' is a fundamental question for every manager to ask.

The dominant indicator of personal effectiveness used by organisations is the concept of **competency**. Competencies are effective behaviours that drive outcomes. The idea is that if certain skills can be developed, this will result in a high level of performance against the goals and targets set by your workplace. It may also be a sustainable advantage in the job market. In fact, competency-based practice is so widespread it would be difficult to find many companies that don't plan, measure and evaluate managerial performance this way. Making a link between skills, effective behaviours and outcomes is one way to find developmental gaps, but it is not the whole story (if only it were that simple). Not everything in management can be reduced to a measurable competency so easily.

> competencies are effective behaviours that drive outcomes

If you are intending to get on in your career, explore new directions or even look for a way out, then a thorough re-evaluation of personality type and perception is a start. My experience with MBAs has shown me that a more thought-provoking question to ask is: Where are you in your life cycle? This is because the answer must involve you looking at yourself in relation to the world to understand your identity and purpose.

Purpose: What is my contribution?

Personal development is the process of advancing identity and self-knowledge, of developing talents, potential and employability across our lifespan. It involves us acknowledging where we are in the present, and sometimes letting go of things from our past. In Chapter 1 you were asked to reflect on why you had picked up this book. Did you identify a sense of challenge at work or a need to move on in your career? Would it have made sense for you to think about these things five or ten years ago? Why not leave it until later in your career? Why now?

ACTIVITY FOR REFLECTION

Life chapters

This is a great exercise to do in order to identify patterns in your life and perhaps signals of what to let go.

Imagine your life as if it were a book, with each stage or part its own chapter. First try to draw a timeline to identify these stages and key events or turning points. Then write a title and short summary for each chapter and include, if you can, transitions from one chapter to the next. Your 'book' is unfinished, but you may now be able to identify patterns and recurring themes.

What it means to be an adult is not a simple question. Danish-American psychiatrist Erik Erikson viewed life as a cycle from birth to death with eight stages of development. As we go through life, biology, cognitive development and – crucially – the social environment combine to trigger various struggles. Erikson called them 'crises', which we must deal with in order to understand a particular core value. The best known of Erikson's psychosocial transitions is probably the 'identity crisis' of adolescence. Less well known are the three further stages of adulthood (see Figure 2.1). It is those adult periods that cover your career.

We leave adolescence and enter young adulthood, where our concern is learning what (and who) we care for. This is a formative period in our lives, one where we build relationships and families. Erikson believed that from our mid-30s to our early 60s we move to mature adulthood, where we are inevitably drawn outward to the question of our productivity and how we shape the world around us. At this stage, we face a crisis between 'generativity', or the extension of love into the future, and 'stagnation', which is this energy

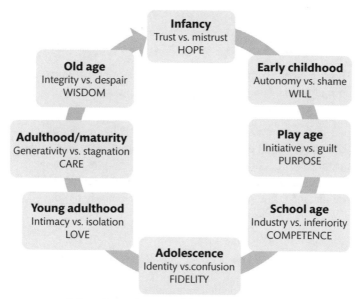

FIGURE 2.1 Erikson's psychosocial life cycle model of development
Source: Adapted from Erikson, E. (1994) *Identity and the Life Cycle*, W.W. Norton & Co. Ltd. Reproduced with permission.

selfishly turned in to please only ourselves. Are we able to balance this societal role and this concern with how the world is for future generations and still leave time and space for ourselves? This is the personal context for management. If you can work through this, understanding both sides of the conflict, it can make it incredibly productive.

CASE STUDY

The Gates Foundation – generativity and the life cycle

In 1975 Bill Gates and Paul Allen co-founded Microsoft. Nearly 40 years on, the computer software giant was the world's largest software maker by revenue and one of the world's most valuable companies.

While his company continues to maintain long-term prosperity, it may ultimately be that a legacy will be felt more through the work of the Gates Foundation than in software development. Set up by Bill and his wife Melinda in 1997, the Foundation has been boosted by sizable donations from US investor Warren Buffett from 2006 onwards, and in June 2014 had an asset trust endowment of $38 billion. It has made almost $30 billion in grants since its inception. In the US the foundation works to improve school education and elsewhere the main types of projects supported are in global health (vaccination, immunisation and disease eradication) and global development (education, agriculture, family planning and sanitation). In fact, Bill Gates expects to give away 95 per cent of his net worth during his lifetime.

The couple first discussed the idea and purpose of the Foundation during a holiday to Africa in 1993, when he was 38 and she was 28. In March 2014 Bill and Melinda were interviewed at a TED conference about their work and the early days of the Foundation.[3] At one point, Bill says, 'We had a certain enthusiasm that that would be the phase, the post-Microsoft phase would be our philanthropy', to which Melinda adds, 'Which Bill always thought was going to come after he was 60, so he hasn't quite hit 60 yet, so some things change along the way.'

Gates brings to the work of the Foundation many of the qualities that drove innovation in Microsoft, in particular a view of learning as a continuous activity. Unusually Bill and Melinda decided they do not want their Foundation to exist in perpetuity and it will wind down and spend all its assets within 20 years of their deaths. 'We can try and solve the problems of today,' believes Bill. 'The next generation will have to decide what the problems are they want to tackle.'[4]

Bill Gates, of course, has means at his disposal to amplify the possibilities of generativity. But in smaller ways, we all begin to face questions in this period of our lives after we have met the challenges of the first phase of adulthood. It's easy to see how the life-cycle concept maps onto the challenges of moving from middle to senior management (you can compare this with Jim Collins' thoughts on leadership in Chapter 10).

Practice: What action should I take?

What are your goals? A lot of people have a hunch that something needs to change but cannot accurately say what that is, and we often set goals for ourselves that are vague or not compelling. As we established in the previous chapter, management is a purposive activity; it has an end in mind. So it helps to have developmental goals that are expressed in positive language. For example, writing down SMART goals, an idea developed from the work of Peter Drucker, is a good exercise for this. SMART stands for:

Specific: Is it snappy and positive (and a move *towards* something)?

Measurable: What evidence will indicate you have reached it?

Achievable: Have you got, or can you get, the resources you need?

Relevant: Is the goal in harmony with the bigger picture? Consider the impact of your goal on your family, work and community. Consider, too, what would happen if you didn't reach it.

Time bound: By when? Without a timeframe, your goal remains a nicely worded dream.

ACTIVITIES FOR REFLECTIVE PRACTICE

1 Write down, in as much detail as you can:

    (a) One short-term work or career goal.

    (b) One medium-term work or career goal.

    (c) One long-term career goal.

2 Share and discuss these goals with another person. For each, also tell another person the first concrete action you will take towards each (telling someone else increases the likelihood of it happening).

Work–life balance is about having a say in when, where and how you work, and recognising that it is healthy to try to achieve a fulfilling life both inside and outside work. Having your view accepted and respected by others (organisations, families and society as a whole) is important in avoiding too much stress or burn-out.

How to get more balanced

While there are no hard and fast rules about how a person should divide up their lives, most of us will recognise a few major categories such as health, levels of attainment at work or in our career, relationships with those closest to us, and an inner world of self-actualisation and purpose. Our lives are full of tensions, dilemmas and choices, both at work and at home.

> our lives are full of tensions, dilemmas and choices

A great way of seeing how things are balanced in your life is in a wheel of life, a diagnostic tool developed for coaching. Constructing your own wheel is a great way to identify and perhaps surprise yourself about where you need to put your energies. Figure 2.2 shows a blank version. You can re-create your own with labels such as 'physical environment', 'family and friends', 'career', 'money', 'health', 'recreation', 'significant other/spouse', 'spirituality', the choice is yours. To create your own wheel of life, first select eight aspects of your life that are important to you and use each to label a segment. Decide, on a scale of 1–10, how satisfied you are at the moment with each. Then colour in your own chart and (preferably in conversation with someone else) identify which one needs action now. It might not be the one with the lowest score.

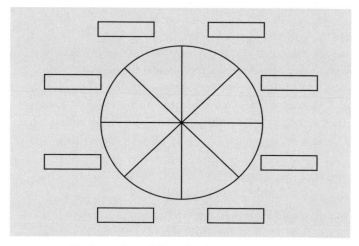

FIGURE 2.2 Blank version of the wheel of life

The wheel is one of the most versatile prompts for noticing what's absent. You can even create variants that go deeper. How about a 'wheel of personal goals', or 'wheel of stress', or even a 'wheel of priorities'? No wonder coaches love using it with clients.

Coaching is still developing as a profession and is also now seen as a skill that managers need to have. Top executive coach Alison Hardingham, in her book *The Coach's Coach*, has this definition, as someone who:

> helps another person or group of people articulate and achieve their goals, through conversation with them. Coaching happens whenever that happens; and it happens all the time, not just in meetings with people who carry the title of 'coach'.[5]

Managers should not be in a formal coaching relationship with their subordinates, but a coaching mindset energises and refocuses and can be used in many different contexts. Managers often comment that their general approach to building and developing relationships improves as they coach and are coached by others. At the heart of the coaching is the ability to build rapport with another person. One useful framework for this is the GROW model developed by John Whitmore.[6] This is a structured process for setting and clarifying development goals:

Goal: Dig or mine for topics and objectives that will challenge and engage you, and that will deliver real value for you, your organisation or the community you live in.

Identify two or three primary goals and add a 'shine' to each – shape each one with a wording that makes it feel real and exciting. Your goals should inspire you and they should produce an emotional response in you.

Reality: Where are you now? What is the gap between this and where your goal sits? What is pushing you towards your goals? What is stopping you? Your reality changes all the time. As you move towards your goal, your reality moves as well.

Options: These are alternatives, choices. Not choices for alternative goals but choices on what actions you can take to move towards your goals.

Will: The final step is to commit to action. Any procrastination or lack of motivation should be noted (it may be there for a reason). The GROW model is not linear.

Finding tools to use in your career development

Early in your career there is a strong case for a competency-based view of skills acquisition, and for using personality assessment tools in a methodical and measurable way. But experience has taught me that these are less useful the more you progress and the older you get. Your skills and competencies become more fluid with experience.

One good stepping stone between the two comes from Stephen Covey's book *The 7 Habits of Highly Effective People*.[7] This is a great set of questions to challenge yourself to take control of your personal development. Covey wants you to go from being dependent on others for your learning to independence (taking responsibility for yourself) through to interdependence (integrating with your context). This follows the same development in thinking as *The Every Day MBA*.

▌ **Habits 1 to 4**: going from dependence to independence:

  – Be pro-active: take responsibility for your personal development.

- Begin with the end in mind: 'if you don't know where you are going, any road will take you there' is the saying.
- Put first things first: categorise tasks by importance, not urgency.
- Think win-win: seek solutions to problems that benefit others as well as yourself.

▌**Habits 5 to 7**: moving from independence to interdependence:

- Understand first, before trying to be understood: shut up and listen. You will learn from others.
- Synergise: creativity comes from combining ideas. Innovation is one of the emergent properties of this.
- Sharpen the saw: a mental attitude of constant improvement, life-long learning.

You need to shift focus from you just as a separate individual to you as an integrated part of a complex system.

Putting it together: approaching management with an open mind

Management in the middle levels of organisations demands and rewards the efficient use of limited resources to meet short-term targets. Organisations will, on the whole, promote skills for problem solving and closure. This is stressful, if only because technology, internationalisation and economic recessions have a tendency to produce more work, not less. To be a better manager or leader you need breakthrough management practice, which requires two things:

1 Self-awareness, self-knowledge and reflective practice.

2 Understanding of the complexity and uncertainty of the business environment and all the things that can affect the short-term goals.

That is what MBA thinking develops. In the remainder of the book, we start to explore how this world operates. You will continue to be asked questions designed to improve your reflective practice. In addition, at the end of each chapter there will be one or two personal development questions for you to consider.

Further reading

A classic text:	*How to Win Friends and Influence People* by Dale Carnegie (2006), Vermillion. First published in 1937, this book certainly counts as a classic and is still relevant.
Going deeper:	*Quiet: The power of introverts in a world that can't stop talking* by Susan Cain (2013), Penguin Books. Cain's book is a refreshing examination of a side of leadership and management we often don't hear about.
Watch this:	Video extract of psychiatrist Viktor Frankl being interviewed in 1977 about his beliefs about the search for meaning: **www.youtube.com/ watch?v=YpN2D_tGsiY**

Notes

1 Schön, D.A. (1983) *The Reflective Practitioner: How professionals think in action*, Jossey-Bass.

2 Rath, T. (2007) *StrengthsFinder 2.0*, Gallup Press.

3 www.ted.com/talks/bill_and_melinda_gates_why_giving_away_our_wealth_has_ been_the_most_satisfying_thing_we_ve_done, TED Conferences LLC. Quote reproduced with permission.

4 www.gatesfoundation.org, Bill and Melinda Gates Foundation. Quote reproduced with permission.

5 Hardingham, A. (2004) *The Coach's Coach: Personal development for personal developers*, Chartered Institute of Personnel and Development.

6 Whitmore, J. (2009) *Coaching for Performance: GROWing human potential and purpose – the principles and practice of coaching and leadership*, 4th Edition, Nicholas Brealey Publishing.

7 Covey, S. (2007) *The 7 Habits of Highly Effective People*, Simon & Schuster.

Tactical MBA thinking: how to organise resources

Tactic, n. [ˈtaktɪk] a method used or a course of action
followed in order to achieve an immediate or short-term
aim

The conventional view of tactics is that they are what
you use to deliver strategy. Tactical thinking includes
the day-to-day implementation of agreed goals and
describes the kind of decision making that adjusts to the
problems, dilemmas and choices every manager meets as
they do their job. What you do in those moments to keep
your head above water is tactical and this thinking occupies
the majority of a middle manager's day. It involves:

▌ organising the resources in a business to create value
(remember, this is every manager's aim)

▌ using multiple methods for observation and measurement
and repeated cycles of trial and error

▌ making incremental improvements (not re-inventing the
wheel)

▌ communication

▌ short- to medium-term planning and making relatively
reversible decisions.

Tactical thinking uses a sequential or lineal approach. If
tactics are not aligned to the strategy of the organisation
then the strategy can quickly come unstuck, and when
this happens lower levels of management can find
themselves trapped in office or corporate politics. There
are three types of resource essential to creating value in a
company:

1 processes and operations, and how they are planned and
improved

2 people, and what they do

3 money, and the microeconomics behind financial
decisions.

Tactical thinking is a bit like navigating towards a
destination on a sailing ship. You are clear about where you
are heading, but your course is affected by changing winds
and by the movements of currents in the sea around you.
You keep on course by constantly adjusting sails to get the
most out of the conditions. The people, the processes and
the cash in your business are a bit like the sails on a ship. In
this part we will see in turn how each of these resources is
organised as a function.

Processes and operations

'Begin at the beginning,' the King said, very gravely,
'and go on till you come to the end: then stop.'

Lewis Carroll, *Alice in Wonderland*

In a nutshell

All managers are day-to-day operations managers. Whether in the private or public sector, in for-profit or not-for-profit, large or small organisations, at the top or the bottom, almost every aspect of management can be seen as a contribution to activities that are organised, planned and subject to evaluation. In short, they manage processes that make up the operations that deliver the goods and services.

In this chapter you will:

▌ learn about the background, context and scope of the operations function

▌ define the difference between tactical and strategic management of operations

▌ apply the input–transformation–output model to processes

▌ explore supply chain management

'Doing' is a process

Processes are activities that transform inputs to outputs. An operation may consist of many processes. For an MBA it is essential to know something about processes and operations because:

▌ No other subject gets this close to analysing what an organisation does. Doing what you do well may be the only difference between you and your competitors.

▌ Equally, the operations function has a strong claim for being where future strategy is translated into present activity. All strategy must at some point be turned into a process that works.

This is a function always with one eye on today and another on tomorrow.

ACTIVITIES FOR REFLECTIVE PRACTICE

1 Contact someone in your network and arrange to visit some of the operations of their organisation. Be curious and ask questions while you are there and later write a reflective account of what you saw. Compare with the processes you know. What was different? What was similar? What made you stop and think?

2 Identify a known issue facing your business about which you can make a prediction. How will that issue affect how the business operates?

These questions illustrate the all-pervasive nature of operations and process management and the tension between how things are best organised now versus what needs to be planned to prepare for the future. These twin tasks form the context for the management of processes and operations.

Herend Porcelain, Hungary

For many centuries, the art of making true porcelain, known as white gold, had eluded Europeans, until the founding of the Meissen works in 1710. The massive demand for fine porcelain fuelled a boom in suppliers in Germany, France and central Europe that peaked in the nineteenth century.

Anyone visiting Herend porcelain manufactory in western Hungary today would be forgiven for thinking that they had stepped back in time about 150 years to that earlier phase of the industrial revolution. Very little has changed in how decorative ceramics are produced since the company was founded in the 1830s. In quiet, well-lit workshops, fragrant with turpentine, rows of painters and master-painters hand-mix colours and then painstakingly apply patterns to forms that have been hand-moulded by throwers and master throwers, and glazed and fired by specialist craftspeople.

Herend has had many ups and downs over the years, but is now a thriving and profitable business. The manufactory is not a living museum; it is a high-end luxury goods company and the largest producer of hand-painted porcelain in the world. Turnover in 2012 was €17 million with a net profit of €2.8 million. It employs more than 770 staff and 75 per cent of the company is owned by them. Many expect to work at Herend their whole lives, following in the footsteps of parents and grandparents. A college on-site trains the next generation in the skills needed to carry on the traditional craft (it takes seven years to qualify fully as a painter, for example).

Because there are only three basic raw materials and almost no automation, Herend is an ideal place to study the rudiments of processes and operations. In principle, the thinking needed here is the same required in any system that transforms input to output.

Everything Herend makes is manufactured to order, every step performed by a specialist, and every piece signed by the painter who finished it. Customers can, in theory, order literally millions of products by combining 15,000 forms with 2,000 decors, in 7 categories. On-site, which works at full capacity, people are busy but nothing is rushed. The company takes great pride in empowering and involving its employees in quality improvement. Herend was awarded ISO 9001 certification in 1995 and has implemented ISO 14001 for environmental management, working to 132 Key Performance Indicators derived from strategy.[1]

Herend has no interest in growing beyond what it considers to be its current sustainable size, except in the margin it makes from sales.[2]

Herend's gentle pace of operations may look like the antithesis of the hectic and high-tech world of modern organisations. But look again. Herend occupies and exploits a market niche, profitably, with attention to detail, quality and customer needs, and the pace at which it works actually makes it an interesting illustration of the principles of operations and process management, slowed down.

The context of managing processes and operations

It is useful to take the process view to understand a business because the effective and efficient management of operations is what generates value for the organisation. Tactical decision making in operations management is aimed at maintaining the capacity to meet the current needs and satisfy customers and stakeholders. To achieve this, operations management tends to break things down to constituent parts. Accordingly, operations management is about the design, implementation, evaluation and improvement of the systems that deliver goods, products or services of a business in the here and now. First-level managers typically focus on small-scale processes or single steps in bigger operations and may find themselves working purely at this level in their functional area. Strategic decision making, at the other end, looks at providing goals for the future needs and senior managers have to see how the types of process make sense in the context of the organisation as a whole. The responsibility for bridging this capacity gap sits with middle managers.

> the responsibility for bridging this capacity gap sits with middle managers

As a middle manager you may be given responsibility for groups of steps, or entire complex processes. Operations management will involve the design, implementation, evaluation and improvement of processes that bridge the gap between the present and the future. Managers at this level have the sometimes difficult task of doing two things at once – aligning to strategic plans and requirements set from above, while making sure the current set up runs smoothly. Although the tactical and strategic levels (the short term and longer term) should work in harmony, in reality this is far from easy. There are several reasons for this:

▌ **Language and culture**: different organisations – and parts inside an organisation – define processes and their boundaries in different ways. Finding a common language, dealing with politics and navigating the unwritten rules of how an organisation functions all require time and effort.

▌ **Complexity**: the more processes are grouped together, the higher the level of complexity.

▌**Uncertainty**: the more an organisation projects into the future, the less it can be certain about where, when and how value will be generated.

When managing processes, some prefer what British researcher Peter Checkland called a 'hard systems' approach, which uses an engineering mindset and simplifies the model of the system to lineal cause and effect.[3] Here, many people just enjoy 'getting on with the job' in a nuts and bolts sort of way. By contrast, a 'soft systems' approach sees problems as ill-defined and process in terms of the varied views of all concerned. In practice, both approaches constitute the various models in use today.

Input, transformation, output (ITO): process mapping

There are three basic organising concepts needed for any process:

Inputs: which are either resources being transformed or resources being used to transform. For example, in a winery the grapes used to make a wine are the resources that are being transformed. In contrast, the knowledge required to judge the right time to harvest the grapes, the people who work in the winery, the vats, barrels and bottles in which the wine matures, and the money borrowed from the bank are all inputs used to transform something else. Inputs can be physical or abstract and may come from elements outside the organisation such as suppliers.

Transformation: or the part of the process where value is added by, for example, a material transformation or a change in physical location, ownership, or purpose and use. In the winery this might involve not just the time it takes for the wine to ferment but also the management of the expectations of customers (perhaps in terms of branding).

Outputs: goods and services, as well as any waste or by-products from the transformation step. Outputs may be for external or internal customers, or other processes. Outputs, in the winery, would include the wine in labelled bottles, and also the residues from cleaning the equipment or the skins from the grapes.

Highly structured processes in assembly-line manufacturing, such as the automotive industry, have provided much of the background and terminology used in operations management. But even if you're managing in a company whose products are intangible services, what you do can be understood in terms of inputs, transformations and outputs.

Process maps and rich pictures

When you need to get detail, a visual way of mapping the passage of any good or service is by using process flow charts. There are some generally accepted symbols used for these, which can be a useful starting point for defining, describing and analysing exactly how your business works – see Figure 3.1.

Process flow charts can be made at three levels:

1. **High-level:** covers the major events in the process only.
2. **Detailed:** has every step mapped, including decision points, queues and feedback loops.
3. **Swim-lane:** extends to show detail of actions by the multiple roles in the process.

Process flow charts are OK for constructing the flow of an operation at a very broad level but can quickly become bogged down in technical detail if you try to map everything that happens or could happen. They are also limited in

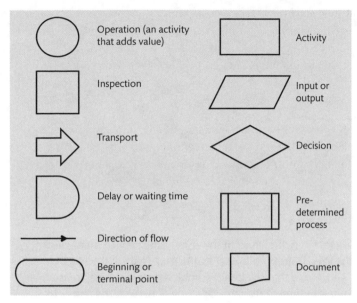

FIGURE 3.1 Standard set of process flow symbols

identifying issues that are not part of a process. Rich pictures, developed by systems thinker Peter Checkland, are a fantastic way to gather information about a complex situation (see Figure 3.2, for example). Using drawings or pictures to think about issues frees your mind to create links and associations and to see patterns. Rich pictures can uncover not just how processes work but also how people see them. Symbols are used, but much more freely. There are few rules in how to create one, but the instructions in the second activity below may guide you.

> using drawings or pictures to think about issues frees your mind to create links

FIGURE 3.2 A rich picture of the role of the service manager in the West London Mental Health Trust (part of the NHS in the UK), a role that sits between half a dozen service areas in hospitals in three boroughs. Drawing it allowed the teams to acknowledge 'the barrage of radio waves of communication coming down, and how exhausting it must be to absorb and filter what is passed further down the chain'

ACTIVITIES FOR REFLECTIVE PRACTICE

1 For your organisation, or the part in which you work, construct a high-level transformation flow diagram (only the main processes). Then:

   (a) Discuss and refine your diagram with other managers in your organisation.

   (b) Note how and when in the operation there are feedback loops.

2 Create a rich picture of your role at work. Colours, images and metaphors are encouraged. Have fun drawing it, but make sure the elements are connected. Use words only when a picture won't work.

(a) Start with structure (the parts of the situation that are stable).

(b) Then look for what moves in the process (e.g. activities).

(c) Pay attention to how they interact with each other but try not to get stuck in theoretical functional silos. Rich pictures should show how things actually are.

(d) Don't forget feelings, emotions and behaviour. Include yourself in the picture.

Which of these two mapping methods did you most prefer?

Types of processes

Manufacturing operations can be broken into five process types to reflect how much flexibility is needed in either the process or the product. These are as follows:

▌ **Ad hoc project**: one-off, customised or occasional projects. These can take a long time to complete and may themselves contain the other process types. The 2012 London Olympics was an ad hoc project, for example.

▌ **Job shop**: high variety but low volume, jobbing processes are ready to provide a wide range of products or services with little repetition. Specialist precision toolmakers, London's bespoke tailors in Savile Row and online greetings card provider Moonpig.com are examples.

Then there are three sorts of flow:

▌ **Batch**: longer runs with less variety than job lots. Outputs are similar but may be large or small in number (a village baker produces small batches of bread, modern agricultural methods can produce very large batches of chickens).

Line: high-volume manufacture or assembly of standardised components. The automotive assembly process is a familiar example, as would be the majority of garment production in much of the world.

Continuous: largely automated, very high volume with relatively high costs associated in set-up and cessation. A Pepsi bottling plant, for example, will run at high speed and continuously for high volumes of a small variety of products.

The operations function in any organisation may be geared to achieving one of two things:

1. **Agility**, that is, the ability for the whole organisation to respond with speed to major changes in the environment or in demand.

2. **Lean**, which is the goal of an operations process that has eliminated all waste in input, transformation or output.

Service-sector processes and operations fall into three types of process:

Professional: high variety, low volume, where a long time may be spent in contact between provider and customer. Lawyers, doctors and bespoke technical support or consulting are examples.

Service 'shop': most of our service interactions involve some customisation, but are essentially held within limits of variety. Buying something in a shop, renting a car or staying in a hotel are services that all fit into this category.

Mass: many customer transactions with almost no customisation. The provider of the service needs little judgement to do their job and the customer may be going through a routine. In mature economies, many of these services are now automated (for example, self-service supermarket checkouts, airport self-service check-ins).

Supply chain management

Supply chain management is oversight (i.e. planning and control) of the relationships between the various activities of the 'journey' of goods and services to customers. It may involve elements such as procurement that are outside the direct control of the organisation. The overall idea is that the manager needs to ensure that all this ends up with some value added, usually expressed in terms of margin or profit. It is not always such a simple task, however, partly because the meaning behind the concept of value is, as we have seen, in the eye of the beholder.

A supply chain network consists of all the components that are needed to source, transform and deliver what an organisation makes or does to its customers. It includes not just the physical locations and proprietary logistical or support systems but also the contracts and agreements with first- and second-tier suppliers of raw materials, outsourced functions which are part of value creation, and methods of evaluation of customer satisfaction. All these aspects need decision making that remains alert to the strategic goals of the organisation, the behaviours of competitors and stakeholders, economies of scale, and impacts on fixed costs and investment.

The idea that operations cross the boundaries of all primary, support and managerial activities was captured by Michael Porter in the supply chain model (see Figure 3.3) in the 1980s. Today this still remains an influential, integrating model.

Porter expected this tool to be used in decision making specifically to exploit competitive advantage, but it is often used now for justifying the structures and relationships between primary and support functions in organisations.

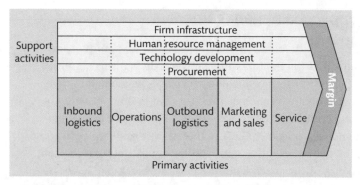

FIGURE 3.3 Michael Porter's value chain framework
Source: Porter, M.E. (2004) *Competitive Advantage*, Free Press. With the permission of The Free Press, a Division of Simon & Schuster, Inc., all rights reserved.

Measuring supply chain success

One widely used framework you may find useful for evaluating process management is the Supply Chain Operations Reference (SCOR), developed by the Supply Chain Council (SCC).[4] It summarises the language and definitions used in the design of the supply chain and allows users to model a process, benchmark performance against KPIs (Key Performance Indicators), as well as learn from others' *best practice*. There are five basic types of process in SCOR, each one a relationship between a supplier and a customer:

1. **Source**: all procurement and delivery, including from your supplier's supplier to your supplier.

2. **Make**: adding value in production through transformation of goods and services.

3. **Deliver**: to the customer of the goods or services.

4. **Plan**: preparation, oversight and management of all links in the chain.

5. **Return**: handling reverse flow, usually from complaint or default after delivery.

How to measure process: flow, inventory and capacity

Sensible process measurements are important for planning, control and improvement. Let's consider the fundamentals:

▌ **Flow** is measured in the throughput time, or how long it would take to perform a given process on a product or service with no delays or waiting along the way.

▌ **Capacity** is the throughput rate, measured as how many or how much of something can be processed within the resources allocated for it.

Whatever is sitting around in between transformative processes on its way to the customer is referred to as inventory, or work in progress.

Lead times, or the delays between initiating and completing an order, can be deliberately longer than process times, and sometimes much longer than they should be. The delivery time refers to how long something actually takes and this may be much longer than the process time (flow). Generally, the shorter you can make the delivery time, the more efficient, or leaner, your process will be and the greater the amount of feedback from more iterations of the process you will get. Because of the delicate relationship between supply, demand and price, any change in capacity – which can lead or lag demand – requires careful consideration and planning. One way of smoothing the ups and downs in supply–demand capacity changes is through inventory management. Here, though, there are other risks, such as what your competitors are doing and what additional capital costs might be incurred.

Little's Law, a mathematical relationship, is often used to show the relationship between these three elements of an operation:

throughput time (flow) = work in progress (inventory)/
throughput rate (capacity)

Different businesses will denote different types of units in
flow management (e.g. producers, customers, cash, etc.),
but the principle has proved very adaptable for many stable
processes. For example, at an airport check-in, from the
passenger's perspective value is a function of i) how long it
takes to walk up to a counter and for the official to make a
decision (throughput time), ii) how many desks are manned
(capacity) and iii) how many people are in the queue doing
nothing (work in progress). However, other stakeholders,
working from exactly the same data, may derive a
completely different evaluation of value added.

Planning, control and feedback

Every operation requires some form of measurement.
Operational measurement can be part of a planning process
to encourage radical progress in a new direction. In terms
of control it could be used to identify where there are gaps
between current performance and targets or benchmarks, or
simply to confirm where things stand at a given moment. In
such cases, managers often look to identify bottlenecks. In
response to the lean movement, the Theory of Constraints
(TOC) was developed by Eliyahu Goldratt to show the
business case for how every effort should be made to manage
to the narrowest point in a system, as opposed to the idea of
managing quality at every stage (see below).[5]

Quality: measurement, evaluation and improvement

Quality control probably has ancient roots in buyers
checking what suppliers were selling them before taking

possession (rather like opening the box of eggs at the supermarket before you pay). As manufacturing technology grew in sophistication, methodical sampling tools such as statistical process control (SPC) were developed to identify defects during production that could pre-empt an end-user's refusal. This quality control phase moved on to the idea of quality assurance and eventually to quality management, which pervades every step and stage of every process in an operation – with the goal of making sampling redundant and the idea of an unhappy customer an impossibility.

One person closely associated with this was the US academic W. Edward Deming, famous for his 'plan-do-check-act' cycle of continuous improvement. Deming inspired the development of high value-added manufacturing in Japan in the 1960s and 1970s. He was famously quoted as saying that 94 per cent of problems in quality are systemic and the responsibility of management, rather than simple instances of error.[6]

A systemic embrace of a 'people' aspect in improving output is core to the concept of total quality management that took hold in the 1980s, even in sectors where the emphasis had been only on the reduction of defective units in production lines. TQM was widely adopted and promoted as a way of cutting cost and waste. It has since been built on as a holistic, organisation-wide effort to reach the same levels of attention to detail attained in manufacturing in every function of a business. Perhaps the most famous example of TQM in action is the 'just-in-time' philosophy of the Toyota Production System (TPS), which was a pre-cursor to the lean manufacturing movement.

> a systemic embrace of a 'people' aspect in improving output is core

ACTIVITIES FOR REFLECTIVE PRACTICE

1 How is quality measured in your work?

2 Revisit your answer to the question at the start of this chapter about a known issue in the future. What do you know that will have an impact on your organisation's readiness? How would you go about communicating this to senior management?

Putting it together: value creation is a process, too

Processes, and the operations they comprise, are basic to the concept of value creation. Every firm will have developed, over time, its own set of procedures. Managing groups of processes in an operation well is a very important aspect of what managers do. Managing those who manage operations represents the coordinated efforts of an organisation to employ models of excellence and these can have a real impact.

It is worth noting that we have adopted a machine metaphor to explain these processes and how they fit together. The real test of this way of thinking is the interface with people. This is notoriously difficult to get right. Improvement initiatives such as business process re-engineering (BPR) have proved unsustainable as times and fashions have changed around them, though successors such as the ISO 9000 series or Motorola's Six Sigma continue to rely on the same paradigm. In addition, a link between this view of operational quality and corporate reputation, in Chapter 11, will present a challenge to the prevailing view.

Further reading

A classic text:	*The Machine that Changed the World* by James Womack, Daniel T. Jones and Daniel Roos (New Edition, 2007), Simon & Schuster. First published in 1990, this book charts the birth of the lean production system in the automotive industry.
Going deeper:	*Operations Management,* 7th Edition, by Nigel Slack (2013), FT Prentice Hall. A really comprehensive overview of the whole topic.
Watch this:	'The evolution of the pit stop' – footage from 1950 and 2013 shows how to improve a process (if you have the money): **http://youtu.be/RRy_73ivcms**

Notes

1 **www.herend.com**
2 There's a video showing the processes and operations at Herend here: **http://bit.ly/1nXWzWe** (You might want to mute the music while you watch.)
3 Checkland, P. and Scholes, J. (2009) *Soft Systems Methodology: A 30-year retrospection,* John Wiley & Sons.
4 **https://supply-chain.org/our-frameworks**, accessed July 2014.
5 Goldratt, E. (1990) *Theory of Constraints,* North River Press.
6 Deming, W.E. (2013) in Orsini, J. (ed.) *The Essential Deming: Leadership principles from the father of quality,* McGraw-Hill Professional.

QUESTIONS FOR REFLECTION

1 Draw a mind map or a rich picture of a personal system that you are part of. This could be your family, a social group you are a member of, or your community. Make a few notes on anything that occurs to you, and remember that explaining your picture to another person can reveal a lot.

2 What would you do in life if money were no object?

People

Hell is other people.

Jean-Paul Sartre

In a nutshell

Businesses are run by people. Great businesses are run by talented people, at all levels. The challenging job of managing this human resource mix belongs to all managers, not only HR professionals or the CEO. Just as with the operations function, your job is to ensure efficient implementation of what is needed right now while at the same time preparing and planning to be able to deliver the future strategy.

Although there is consensus that people are vital to the success of a business, there is no agreement as to what that actually means. This chapter will provide background and structure to what is often a complex topic.

In this chapter you will:

▌ trace the historical development of managing people

▌ examine the external and internal contexts of the HR function

▌ study corporate culture and the evolution of the employment relationship

▌ investigate the role played by people in managing quality

Managing people in a modern organisation

Organisations have always relied on finding, developing and keeping the right staff to carry out all the functions of the enterprise, but what this means in practice has changed in the different eras of management.

▌ **Nineteenth to mid-twentieth century**: the age of the Personnel Department, where people are a resource that can be quantified and costed, their output measured and their recruitment prepared for. This view has its roots in the rapid expansion of workforce need during early and middle stages of the industrial revolution in Europe. Partly in reaction to this new economic model, this revolution was also the age of social reform and the unionisation of labour in many parts of the world.

▌ **From mid-twentieth century**: the age of organisational behaviour (OB) and human resource management (HRM), where people are an essential expression of the culture of the organisation. The entry into the workforce of many more women during the Second World War helped change definitions of labour, and heralded an age in which the development of the transnational or multinational company, sophisticated performance management systems, mass production and, more recently, the shift from manufacturing to service and knowledge-based economies have all played a part. Later, there was mass privatisation and a reduction in unionisation, as well as a movement towards collaboration and empowerment for individuals at work.

▌ **Twenty-first century**: in developed economies, a new age of partnering with stakeholders, fuelled by globalisation and enabled by technology. People are seen as the source of creativity and innovation. Long gone are the days of the monolithic corporate personnel function; HR is now decentralised, and knowledge capital and inter-connectedness are the priorities. In emerging economies, population demographics have begun to exert a drive of their own.

It is the line manager's job to get things done. This is impossible without people, but that presents unique challenges because this is a topic soaked in theories and counter-theories from psychology and sociology. At first, 'people' seems like a topic that lacks the crisp, neat edges MBAs are often so fond of. But, all other things being equal, organisations can be differentiated only by their talent. For this reason, HR has a vital link to strategy.

ACTIVITIES FOR REFLECTIVE PRACTICE

Identify the head of human resources in your organisation. Arrange to interview them if you can.

1 How has their job changed in the last five years?

2 What factors will influence how the organisation manages people in the next five years?

When you have done this, reflect on your own experience managing or being managed by others.

Over the last 25 years line managers have taken direct control of traditional HR functions such as scoping job requirements, running recruitment, performance review and reward, employee motivation and promoting organisational culture. HR professionals are now more likely to act as specialists or consultants to be called on when needed. It is middle management – already under pressure to take on work and respond to every interruption and stimulus –

that has added managing people to an already long list of responsibilities. The result is a core area of management where everyone has first-hand experience (and opinions) but rarely any formal training.

The external context: macro-culture

National culture is often the topic of description and opinion, but rarely of insight. Many organisations now recruit and work across many borders so the need to manage an international, diverse resource has also grown. Perhaps the most famous attempt to study the interplay between regional/national cultural preferences and corporate culture (initially, that of IBM) is by Geert Hofstede.[1] Given the free flow of human resources around the world and the global nature of management as a career, you might think about how these apply (or will apply) to your own experience.

> many organisations now recruit and work across many borders

There are six dimensions of values in his theory:

Power distance: How a society handles inequality in the distribution of power and resources. Large power distance accepts hierarchies in which everyone has and knows their place. In low power distance countries, people look for equality and minimisation of power.

Individualism vs. collectivism: Which takes prominence, the 'I', or the 'we'? Individualism is a preference for looking after your immediate circle. Collectivism stands for a tighter expectation of loyalties to an extended family or wider social networks.

Masculinity vs. femininity: Masculinity as a dimension represents a societal bias for success as being competitive achievement and material rewards. The other aspect, femininity, values success as cooperation and consensus and an aim for quality of life.

Uncertainty avoidance: The extent to which you and those in your society feel uncomfortable with the unknown, or with ambiguity. Hofstede sees this as being an orientation to the uncertainties of the future – resulting in either strong codes of behaviour that do not tolerate dissent (high), or social norms that are more open to 'bending the rules' (weak).

Pragmatic vs. normative: A pragmatic society is one where people accept that there is a lot of complexity in life which may be impossible to explain fully. The purpose of life is to live it, and truth is contextual, material things transient. Under a normative orientation there is a wish to find in explanation the objective 'truth'. Traditions and the past are treasured, spending is encouraged and adaptability is valued.

Indulgence vs. restraint: The sixth, and most recent, dimension contrasts indulgence, in which a society pursues happiness freely as a basic human motive of having fun, with restraint, in which such an urge is regulated or suppressed by social norms.

The interesting thing about culture is that we only really know ours by contrasting it with another. On a small scale this is obvious – we frequently see differences among the people, families and organisations around us. We take a lot of things for granted, and correctly locating our perceptions of the world, especially if we are managers, is much more difficult. Sensitivity to cultural values and norms is important, but as a manager you need to be aware of what is happening in a wider context. Consider how each of the following affects you in your workplace:

The political and legal environment: In the European Union (EU), for example, member countries have agreed to subordinate some national legislative decision making and this has had an effect on employment laws and the free flow of people to work. The legal framework governing ethical behaviour is also important.

Demographics: In the next 50 years the global population will climb to, and probably peak at, 10 billion. Despite a falling fertility rate globally, some countries will struggle to meet the demands of their ageing populations, while others will have to contend with rapidly expanding populations moving into ever-larger urban areas.

Education: Policies that prepare future generations for work require educational systems that align.

Globalisation and international careers: The proven ability to work well across borders and cultures, and in increasingly diverse teams, will be one of the tests for talent management in the future.

ACTIVITIES FOR REFLECTIVE PRACTICE

1 How were you recruited to your current position? Did your organisation take into account any of the macro-level factors above? If you can, go and check your reasoning with your head of HR or line manager.

2 Think about your national culture. Where do you think it sits on each of Hofstede's measures of culture? Now think about the culture of a current or past organisation you know. Is it the same, or different?

We've looked at those things outside the organisation, the ones that set the parameters for how an organisation behaves, and now we will look at the manager's tasks at the organisational level – that is, those things that affect your daily job.

The internal context: organisations and micro-cultures

Details and circumstances may vary from company to company, but when it comes to employing people there are really only two constants that make a difference:

1 A contract of employment between the organisation and the person.

2 The contribution of the contract to our sense of identity, achievement and purpose.

We might spend more than a third of our lives at our places of work so it is no surprise that we feel an attachment that cannot be explained merely by being paid. For many, the idea of culture as a shared set of behaviours feels like common sense.

What is culture? Some describe it as 'the way we do things round here'. The veteran American organisation expert Edgar Schein sees organisational culture as operating below the surface, but evident at three levels:[2]

Level 1 – artifacts: The physical locations, interiors, uniforms (formal or informal) or outward signs of branding.

Level 2 – espoused values: The norms and shared beliefs carried by the employees (articulated occasionally in a mission statement, but often more evident from procedures and rules).

Level 3 – basic assumptions: The sub-conscious of the 'corporate person', deeply held values, the ultimate test being how much tolerance there is for diverse types of behaviours or decision making.

American MBAs place people management under the umbrella of 'organisational behaviour'. It sounds as though an organisation can 'behave' just as an individual person can. This could reflect a pattern in the employment contract between a firm and an individual that is part of the national culture in the US, but actually the idea of OB travels quite well. The organisational design template for many multinational companies follows a similar set of beliefs about hard work, independence and the rights of the individual. It's not hard to see why many managers regard good management of their human resource as a source of competitive advantage (see Chapter 7). However, HR practice is often less than sophisticated. When a human resource issue is mishandled, an otherwise competent manager can find themselves in hot water very quickly, and talented staff can be left demotivated, disillusioned and looking elsewhere.

In fact, studies of what managers actually do at work are a fairly recent phenomenon. It was Henry Mintzberg who pointed out that managers don't spend their time in secluded luxury issuing commands. He observed them being put under pressure, being interrupted and dealing with things as they came up. He did, however, identify three main management roles:[3]

1. **Informational**: internally, sometimes as official spokesperson and sometimes informally, act as mentor and the driver to disseminate communication in the organisation, as well as be the channel for information to the external environment as liaison.

2. **Decisional**: get things moving and implement change projects, adjudicate disputes and handle conflicts or unexpected situations decisively, allocate resources and negotiate with external stakeholders.

3. **Interpersonal**: be a symbolic figurehead or motivational leader, and build a connecting network of information sources external to your organisation.

Managing people means managing the one resource that is everywhere in your organisation. Your ability to analyse the multiple and complex factors influencing this organisational balance is terribly important and it certainly helps to have on hand some tools and techniques to help you cope with this. A robust diagnostic first step for this is to use the McKinsey 7-S framework (see Figure 4.1), a matrix very often applied by MBAs.

> managing people means managing the one resource that is everywhere

The matrix consists of:

Strategy: The overall objectives and the requirements to meet them.

Structure: The hierarchy, organisation of tasks or functions and divisions of labour.

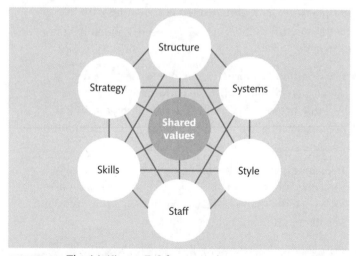

FIGURE 4.1 The McKinsey 7-S framework
Source: Peters, T.J. and Waterman, R.H. (1982) *In Search of Excellence*, McKinsey & Company. Reproduced with permission.

Systems: The processes and operations used to get things done, e.g. the supply chain.

Shared values: The original intention of the organisation, its founding purpose and resulting core beliefs.

Style: More or less equivalent to Schein's level 2 of culture, the unwritten rules.

Staff: The potential represented by the collective of people in the organisation.

Skills: What the organisation (not the individuals in it) is good at.

The 7-S framework is a little harder to apply than it looks because it supposes all the information you need is easily accessible, and clearly some of these factors are intangible. You will also need honesty in admitting where there are internal contradictions in your organisation.

ACTIVITIES FOR REFLECTIVE PRACTICE

Conduct an experiment using the 7-S Framework:

1. In the short term: do any of the seven aspects of culture feel like 'hot spots' in your organisation? Which one would you work on first? Put this analysis on one side for a while, then …

2. In the long term: over time (MBAs always want to do things too quickly; it would be better if they slowed down), develop your understanding of these seven ways of looking at your organisation. You might, for example, revisit your first analysis every six months to see what has changed.

Using McKinsey's 7-S as its framework, Tom Peters and Robert Waterman's 1984 book *In Search of Excellence* for a while was seen as having all the answers when it came to company culture and corporate success.[4] Many of the companies showcased in the book failed in the years that followed, and the lure of culture and 'excellence' as predictors of success faded. The lesson from this is that to understand culture you must link it to performance and value creation (and usually this means the bottom line). The fundamental question remains: how do you as a manager best represent the interests of the founders and owners?

When it comes to managing people, value can be quantified in terms of productivity. The classic ingredients for this are measurement of what people know and what they can do.

Measuring productivity in people management

As we've seen, in the old days HR was about job analysis and the processes needed for selection of personnel with the right qualifications. This is still needed, but what is different is these activities now have to align talent to strategy. The individual desires and wants of employees are not the driver, though shaping the organisational culture means managing a delicate balance between all stakeholders and making everyone feel valued and informed. HR professionals work to exert this cultural influence with three tools:

▌ **Recruitment and retention**: selecting for cultural fit, because 'not fitting in' is arguably a more common reason for leaving a job than a lack of talent or dissatisfaction with pay.

▌ **Training and development**: from induction onwards, training and internal communication need to enable people to understand the cultural norms and engage emotionally.

▌ **Motivation and rewards**: the balance of give and take in an organisation, of which money is only one aspect, is crucial in communicating values and purpose.

These things matter to you, too. A manager is there to get things done, and as soon as the work to be done exceeds the resource available to do it, workforce planning becomes a part of every general manager's role. To undertake this you need to gain a basic understanding (at least) of:

▌ organisational design and structure (luckily, you're in one, so you can at least study that)

▌ job design, recruitment, selection and role development (using the HR professionals to assist and guide, plus your own reflections)

▌ talent retention and management.

CASE STUDY

Cisco

As part of a wider strategic shift in its core business following the 2008 recession, US computing giant Cisco transformed its global HR practices when it created a company-wide shared-services structure, built around 11 cross-functional tactical or strategic pillars.

This extract from an April 2014 article in *Talent Magazine* explains:

> By farming out HR's transactional duties to another department, Cisco says it saved money, freed up talent management professionals to think strategically and boosted employee satisfaction with HR.

> It was the Great Recession, and Cisco Systems' long run of strong business results was in trouble. Sales were shrinking at the data communications pioneer, and executives were keen to cut costs. Out of the crisis emerged a new way of doing the business of HR at Cisco. About two years ago, the company effectively split human resources into tactical and strategic wings. The move put the company

▶

at the forefront of HR design and has yielded other significant benefits.

Employee satisfaction with HR services has held steady or improved, even as Cisco has delivered services 10 per cent more cheaply. In addition, the HR organization has freed up some people management professionals to focus more intently on strategic talent initiatives, such as workforce planning, creating career plans and assigning goals and metrics aligned to the overall business strategy.

It hasn't been easy. The overhaul has required a new mindset among both HR professionals and Cisco's workforce of 75,000 people around the globe. And questions plagued the effort, especially at the outset. 'There was a lot of "FUD" surrounding this when we first started – fear, uncertainty and dread,' said Don McLaughlin, vice president of employee experience at Cisco and one of the architects of the shift. 'We were accused of, "Shared services is going to outsource everything to a business process outsourcing model, we're going to grind the cost out of it, the service is going to be awful, this is going to be a no good, terrible, horrible, very bad thing".' But McLaughlin and his colleagues stuck with their vision, and Cisco's experiment with chopping HR in half suggests the sum of the resulting parts can be greater than the original whole.'[5]

Source: Talent Magazine[6]

Cisco has chosen to centralise its transactional HR functions such as compensation, staffing and learning and development (L&D) into a purely operational 'employee experience' pillar that is shared with IT services. HR strategy, policy and innovation, however, remain part of a specialist HR function. What do you think of Cisco's move?

Performance and reward

HR specialists are probably still the ones, even in smaller organisations, who take first responsibility for recommending financial rewards and they may also oversee the development and deployment of policies to evaluate employee performance. But what these practices and policies look like will vary depending on national location and culture, company history and strategic intent, and without doubt the organisation will want you to pay most attention to performance. When you are in tune with the policies of your organisation, all this can be a very smooth ride. When you're not, it will dramatically interfere with your job, though you will have no one else to blame but yourself if that happens. I'll consider management involvement in performance from three perspectives – motivation, teamwork and the individual's performance.

Motivation: job satisfaction and happiness at work

American psychologist Frederick Herzberg's two-factor theory of motivation and satisfaction prompted a change in how we understand people's engagement with their jobs.[7] Herzberg agreed with the idea that human beings have a set of needs and desires and that achieving these is what motivates us. Abraham Maslow had earlier presented a hierarchy of needs, arranged in a pyramid with basic physiological requirements such as shelter at the base and self-actualisation (never fully defined) at the summit.[8] Herzberg thought, however, that motivation was a bit more complex. Basic needs demotivate us when they are absent but do not add to our happiness when present. Higher-level needs provide true satisfaction and these are what we truly seek. Herzberg saw two independently functioning factors:

▌ **Motivators:** these include being challenged by our work, receiving recognition, achievement or personal growth.

When present in our workplace they give us meaning. They are also all concerned with carrying out tasks. When absent, they tend to make us feel less worthwhile and less competent, which is deeply dissatisfying.

▋ **Hygiene factors**: these are necessary because, when present, they prevent demotivation. However, they do not intrinsically lead to motivation when they are present. Examples include salary, fringe benefits and bonuses, and these will form the context of carrying out tasks, but not what brings us real satisfaction.

If this sounds like common sense, it may be that it is. But like many basic business concepts, 'the devil is in the detail', and in the infinite variation that each particular situation (remember Schön and his swampy lowlands) produces dilemmas for you as a manager. For example, how important do you think praise is for a job well done in motivating a team? In some people and teams it won't be valued, while for others it may be more significant than pay. Maslow and Herzberg's are theories that point to motivation towards desirable goals or ends. Other theories focus on means, or the processes of motivation. Vroom's expectancy theory says that people will choose a way of acting depending on their expectation of the result (the end dictates the means), so managers must remember that motivation is the relationship between effort and result in people's minds.

> how important do you think praise is for a job well done in motivating a team?

It's not a big jump from this to the idea known as the psychological contract (see Figure 4.2), which is a way of measuring how employer and employee see their mutual obligations in employment. At one end of the spectrum it is as a *social exchange*, where psychological well-being, belonging and loyalty are highly valued. At the other end, it is as an *economic exchange*, a transaction of time for money with no expectation of an emotional or long-term attachment.

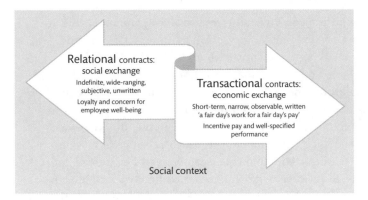

Relational contracts:
social exchange
Indefinite, wide-ranging, subjective, unwritten
Loyalty and concern for employee well-being

Transactional contracts:
economic exchange
Short-term, narrow, observable, written
'a fair day's work for a fair day's pay'
Incentive pay and well-specified performance

Social context

FIGURE 4.2 The psychological contract
Source: Adapted from Rousseau, D.M. (1995) *Psychological Contracts in Organizations: Understanding written and unwritten agreements*, Sage Publications, Inc. Reproduced with permission.

The world of work, however, is undergoing rapid change – a rate of change unprecedented since the very first days of the industrial revolution. We're now used to flat and matrix management structures, the movement of services and jobs around the world, and the pressures on equality and diversity in the workplace, but these are trends from the past acting on the present.

In the future, what will managing people be about? Well, we can expect the following to feature (and also expect some surprises):

▌ lifestyle career choices

▌ gap years at all ages, not just between school and university

▌ lifelong learning

▌ a move from corporate social responsibility to social enterprise (Chapter 11)

▌ social networking

▌ more interest in talent and succession management

▌ a lot more virtual team working.

The last one on this list, teamwork, is a perennial MBA topic, second only to leadership as an object of scrutiny. From talking to executives about their experiences at work, my opinion is that organisations are cautious about the future. They will want managers who are confident with virtual working, willing to be flexible about how and when they work, and committed to putting their personal development goals on hold if possible. Not great news for the self-directed, lifelong learner, who will be looking for balance between work and home. Technology will blur the lines between work and 'life' even more in the future, which means that building networks will be the key skill.

Teams: working with and through others

First-line managers will be expected to demonstrate a willingness to become part of them; middle managers a proficiency in leading them; senior managers a command of the subtleties of managing people in them. With increasingly flat management hierarchies and matrix reporting structures, teams and teamwork have become a ubiquitous feature of large organisations in the last 30 years. Even small to medium-sized enterprises (SMEs) often construct work around them. Teams and groups interest academics, too, and have been studied for decades. Influential psychologist Kurt Lewin coined the term group dynamics in 1945, and the subject has filled the pages of management textbooks ever since.[9] Our study of group covers many scenarios, including a workplace team. All teams must have a specific reason (or charter) for their existence, but there are really two basic types:

1. **Collaborative**: any group whose aim is achievement of one shared goal or output; in other words, the output can be achieved only by working together.

2 **Cooperative**: any group whose aim is for everyone in it to reach their own goal; in other words, each person's goal is personal but will be reached more easily with the help or support of others.

Despite its popularity in organisational settings, the direct benefit of teamwork is hard to measure. In addition, teamwork is quite hard to get right. The model of group formation that has outlived most others is Bruce Tuckman's four-stage model, first developed in the 1950s and shown in Figure 4.3. Tuckman's language has entered management speak as shorthand for any group's theoretical navigation from first contact to task achievement.

American management consultant Patrick Lencioni suggests that teams need to overcome five dysfunctions (each with a remedy below):[10]

1 **Absence of trust**: team members need to be open to each other.

2 **Fear of conflict**: trust allows disagreement and questions.

3 **Lack of commitment**: early conflict and opinion sharing allows for genuine buy-in later on.

4 **Avoidance of accountability**: commitment allows teams to hold each other accountable for decisions and actions.

5 **Inattention to results**: overcoming all of the above lets the team focus on the charter (collective goal).

In the 1980s Meredith Belbin concluded that an effective team needed a balance of different types of behaviours over the life of a project and that different people tended to prefer to play (or to prefer avoiding) a combination of nine team roles.[11] The nine roles are:

Implementer: Someone being disciplined, reliable, conservative and efficient. Turning ideas into practical actions.

Team worker: Someone being cooperative, mild, perceptive and diplomatic. Listening to avert friction.

- Flexibility of approach
- Leadership decided by situation
- Commitment to team success
- Aware of principles/social aspects
- Rewarding and productive

- Feelings not dealt with
- Conformity
- Much talking, little listening
- Weaknesses/mistakes hidden
- No shared view of task
- Defensive against outside threats

Forming
(the undeveloped team)

Performing
(the mature team)

Team dynamics

Storming
(the experimenting team)

Norming
(the consolidating team)

- Confident but not complacent
- Willing to solve team problems
- Handle conflict constructively
- Follow agreed methods, not inflexible
- Interpersonal competence
- Learning and developing

- Review of methods
- Problems faced more openly
- More options considered
- Personal/group issues
- Temporarily more inward looking, more listening

FIGURE 4.3 Tuckman's stages of group development
Source: Adapted from Tuckman, B. (1965) 'Developmental sequence in small groups', *Psychological Bulletin*, 63(6): 384–399. Reproduced with permission of the American Psychological Association.

Plant: Someone being creative, imaginative, unorthodox and solving difficult problems.

Resource investigator: Someone being extrovert, enthusiastic and communicative. Exploring opportunities and developing contacts.

Shaper: Someone being challenging, dynamic and thriving on pressure. Being courageous to overcome obstacles.

Coordinator: Someone being mature, confident, a good chairperson. Clarifying goals, promoting decision making and delegating well.

Monitor evaluator: Someone being sober, strategic and discerning. Seeing all options and judging accurately.

Completer-finisher: Someone being painstaking, conscientious and searching out errors or omissions. Delivering on time.

Specialist: Someone being single-minded, self-starting and dedicated. Providing task-specific knowledge and skills in rare supply.

Tuckman's theory and Belbin's work with management teams in the 1980s and 1990s are examples of the type of modelling of team processes used on MBA programmes. A high-performing team (HPT) is any group that achieves and then exceeds the goals it has been set while at the same time respecting and facilitating the individual objectives of its members. HPTs are difficult to build and even more difficult to maintain, and even Tuckman observed that teams frequently slipped back to earlier stages of formation and that the final 'performing' stage may be short-lived.

Is there anything wrong with this whole approach to teamwork? It might be said that managers often prefer the simple solution to the complex one, even when the complex is the more insightful. In other words, MBAs love short cuts, academics like categorising the world and practitioners enjoy getting results. Theories about teamwork are rarely questioned critically in business schools and while sometimes a shorthand rule of thumb can help, the reality is more complex.

> managers often prefer the simple
> solution to the complex one

Performance of the individual

Traditionally, performance has been about improving employee productivity through systems of motivation and reward, but this is a dynamic field that has changed enormously over the last 30 years in many parts of the world. Changes in legislation covering the rights and responsibilities of employers and employees, expectations of higher economic wealth and also of access to either full-, part-time or flexible working, as well as macroeconomic cycles of relative prosperity and austerity, have all influenced the pay and reward systems organisations use to manage performance.

This topic may appear in an organisation in the following ways:

- **Strategic**: as part of forward planning (and linked to strategy). In practice, many organisations see this as a cycle of activities and processes. It encompasses recruitment, reward and pay, generic training and development, pipeline, talent development and succession planning, and establishment of policies to monitor and maintain standards of process.

- **Tactical**: as part of regular or systematic reviews for individuals delivered usually by line management.

- **Ad hoc**: dealing with situations where something has gone wrong. Unfortunately, this is usually approached in terms of a need to fix the employee rather than a need to fix the system, even though in the majority of cases it is the context that is causing the issue. A great employee can be swallowed up in a poor system.

We've already seen that theories of motivation play a big part in understanding how to manage performance levels, but it remains a difficult concept to measure. Bonus cultures and corporate pension schemes have begun to face more criticism and restrictions, and reward systems in the future may need to find original and flexible mechanisms for remuneration.

ACTIVITIES FOR REFLECTIVE PRACTICE

1 What motivates you at work? What kind of psychological contract is there between you and your organisation?

2 What will be the main challenges in finding, recruiting and motivating staff in your organisation in coming years? You might want to discuss this with senior managers and HR.

Developing an HR strategy

In the previous chapter I said that the operations function always has one eye on managing the present and the other on planning for the future. It should be the same when it comes to managing the people who run, organise and contribute to any organisation. The strategic side of managing people is about two things:

1 Making sure that the right human resources will be in place in the future. This future focus is strategic because it requires hedging against a scarcity of labour. In free-market economies people are free to come and go and – despite constraints of political, social and economic circumstances – organisations must develop policies that will supply quality staff. Globally, the shortage of qualified personnel in the health sector, for example, is so acute that strategic HRM is often a governmental priority.

2 Negotiating the right systems of motivation, rewards and contractual control to meet the uncertainties of a contingent future, and of maintaining a balance in the tension between operating profitably while respecting the rights and responsibilities of employing people around the world.

Strategic HRM in the next 20 years will need to keep pace with the speed of change in other areas of business.

Putting it together: HR takes a Bath

One framework that brings all these messages together in one place, and links them to strategy, is the Bath model of people and performance, shown in Figure 4.4.[12] Concluded from in-depth studies of 12 different companies by a group of researchers based at Bath University, the model was:

▍ an attempt to understand the relationship between all the factors involved in a competitive and sustainable competitive advantage in HR strategy, and

▍ an explanation of the motivational impact of 'discretionary' behaviours on performance.

The research revealed three things:

1 Organisations need to embody their 'big idea' in their HR practices. A clear sense of 'what we stand for' emerges in the relationships between the various elements.

2 Front-line managers are the ones who bring these relationships to life.

3 The 11 policies in the model all link to satisfaction, which links to performance, which in turn is linked to value. But different roles and levels in an organisation need different combinations of those policies.

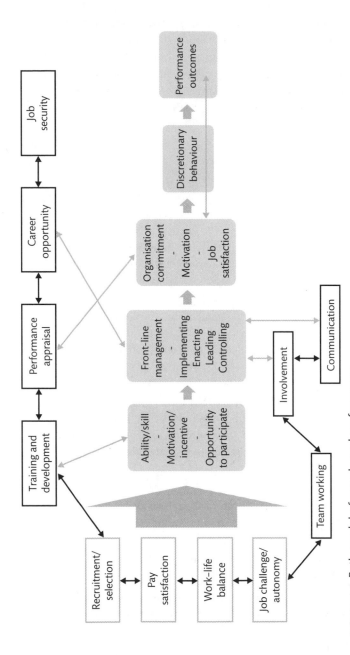

FIGURE 4.4 Bath model of people and performance

Source: Purcell, J., Kinnie, N., Hutchinson, S., Rayton, B. and Swart, J. (2003) 'Understanding the People and Performance Link: Unlocking the Black Box', with the permission of the Chartered Institute of Personnel and Development. London (**www.cipd.co.uk**).

The story of human resource management as a function first went from study of structure to study of culture formed in the structure. Now it is moving again from culture to a study of the relation of culture and structure as a dynamic and open system. The learning organisation is now a byword for good management practice in managing people.

Further reading

A classic text: *The Peter Principle: Why things always go wrong* by Peter, L.J. and Hull, R. (1969), Pan Books. Before Dilbert, there was Peter. It's amazing how this insightful and humorous book, written in another era, still has so much to say that is relevant today.

Going deeper: *Strategy and Human Resource Management* by Peter Boxall and John Purcell (3rd Edition, 2011), Palgrave Macmillan. A comprehensive textbook, pitched at the right level for MBAs and mid-career managers.

Watch this: 'Drive', Dan Pink's engaging 2010 talk on human motivation, animated by the RSA: **www.thersa.org/events/rsaanimate/animate/rsa-animate-drive**

Notes

1 Hofstede, G., Hofstede, G.J. and Minkov, M. (2010) *Cultures and Organizations: Software of the mind*, Third Edition, McGraw-Hill Professional.
2 Schein, E. (2010) *Organizational Culture and Leadership*, 4th Edition, John Wiley & Sons.
3 Mintzberg, H. (1971) 'Managerial work: analysis from observation', *Management Science*, 18(2): B97–B110.
4 Peters, T. and Waterman, R. (2004) *In Search of Excellence: Lessons from America's best-run companies*, 2nd Edition, Profile Books.
5 **www.cisco.com/web/about/ac40/univ/programs/gbs.html**, Cisco Systems, Inc. Quote reproduced with permission.

6 http://talentmgt.com/articles/divide-and-conquer, MediaTec Publishing Inc. Extract reproduced with permission.

7 Herzberg, F., Mausner, B. and Snyderman, B. (1959) *The Motivation to Work*, 2nd Edition, John Wiley.

8 Maslow, A.H. (1943) 'A theory of human motivation', *Psychological Review*, 50(4): 370–396.

9 Lewin, K. (1947) 'Frontiers in group dynamics. I. Concept, method and reality in social science; social equilibria', *Human Relations*, 1: 5–40.

10 Lencioni, P. (2002) *The Five Dysfunctions of a Team: A leadership fable*, John Wiley & Sons.

11 Belbin, M. (2010) *Team Roles at Work*, 2nd Edition, Routledge.

12 Purcell, J., Kinnie, N., Hutchinson, S., Rayton, B. and Swart, J. (2003) *Understanding the People and Performance Link: Unlocking the black box*, Chartered Institute of Personnel and Development.

QUESTIONS FOR REFLECTION

1 How do you describe yourself? Does your job title also function as your identity? If you had to give up your job tomorrow, how would you describe yourself?

2 What sorts of things make you work harder than the minimum?

Finance 1: accounting

Money is better than poverty, if only for financial reasons.

Woody Allen, *Without Feathers*

In a nutshell

This chapter covers the effective use of financial and economic data to support planning, control and decision making for value creation. It's a misconception (albeit a tempting one) that the job of an experienced chief financial officer (CFO) is to find a thousand different ways of saying no. A CFO's job is to agree robust ways of saying yes to value creation and their caution is usually because they are custodians of the resource that is our store and measure of value: money.

Accounting can be jargon-heavy and is highly regulated, but you do not need to know everything a CFO or accountant knows to work alongside the financial experts. When you understand something of the tools and principles of accounting and finance, it is directly applicable to the work you do and you will be better equipped to justify and defend your use of the organisation's resources to achieve its goals.

In this chapter you will:

▋ learn the difference between management and financial
accounting

▋ study economic theory at the level of individuals and
organisations

▋ understand the importance of the time value of money

▋ evaluate an organisation's performance using financial
statements

The basis of accounting

Before diving into an alphabet soup of ratios and economic
formulas, the best place to start is with what managers
actually do day to day. Yours is a world of decisions and
actions, but the logic behind many of an organisation's plans
comes from economic theory. The language and practice
of accounting are designed to measure the performance of
decision making and so all the information provided in this
view of accounting is historical. In other words, it comes
from looking back. There are two broad areas of accounting:

▋ **Management accounting** has an internal audience. It is
about the planning and decision making required to meet
given objectives and is linked to microeconomic theory
(the economics of individual actions). As a part of this,
cost accounting establishes budgets linking detailed
activities in the short-term future to various types of cost.
Most managers are involved in preparing, managing and
then tracking variances in budgets.

▋ **Financial accounting** uses data from past performance to
analyse and interpret where you are in the present and to
gauge the current viability of your business. Accounts have
to be produced by all limited-liability companies. They

summarise and consolidate all the activities from the last year and express them as numbers. Financial accounting thus presents the outcomes of the decisions made in management accounting in a way that is consistent and comparable. In *The Every Day MBA* we're going to use the published accounts of a major UK grocery retailer, Morrisons, to illustrate some of the main aspects of this part of accounting.

I will begin with management accounting, then look at financial accounting, in order to see in more detail the differences between them.

CASE STUDY

Morrisons supermarkets: introduction

With just over 11 per cent share of the UK grocery retail market, Morrisons is a FTSE 100 company and the fourth largest supermarket chain in a fiercely competitive sector. Its main competitors are Tesco, Sainsbury's and Asda (part of Wal-Mart).

From its home base in the north of England, Morrisons expanded when it purchased the assets of its rival Safeway in 2008, doubling in size and gaining a nationwide network of superstores. Morrisons' value proposition is built around a vertically integrated supply chain (it owns all the farms and warehousing that supply its fresh produce) and an in-store format that is deliberately reminiscent of a traditional British high street or market.

Most Morrisons stores are in large, out-of-town sites and it has lagged behind its competitors, which have moved away from this format in recent years by investing in smaller, urban convenience stores. Unlike its three main rivals, in a channel valued at £31 billion annually, Morrisons has developed no online order and delivery service. This is changing. At the end of 2013, it announced a strategic make-or-buy decision to partner with online retailer and delivery company Ocado during 2014. Morrisons also began an ambitious, if belated, expansion into smaller, express grocery stores in prime high-street locations (mostly in units vacated by the video rental company Blockbuster).

According to Morrisons' own estimates, online sales are due to grow by 98 per cent in the next five years, so the challenge is for the whole organisation to realign itself to two new ways of doing business during and after 2014.[1]

Management accounting

In buying this book you made a decision. You incurred a cost, which was balanced with an expectation of a benefit that would be worth something in return. You could have done other things with your money, so the chances are you weighed up any benefits relative to, for example, buying a different book, or a meal, or perhaps using the money to pay off a debt. That is a small example; a much bigger one could be the cost of signing up for an MBA, which is why managers often spend years thinking about it. Getting the most out of limited resources is always an issue. In organisational settings, when it's someone else's money, you need to show judgement and rigor in the decisions you make because they will usually have an effect on the bottom line.

> you need to show judgement and rigor in the decisions you make

Economic activities need to align with organisational goals. Every organisation has limited resources – it can't do everything and what it can do usually can't be done all at once. Remembering the twin roles of management from

Chapter 1 (standing in place of the owners and the ethical creation of value), you begin to see – regardless of whether it's the monthly budget or 10-year capital expenditure – how financial information can help you move from being a re-active to a pro-active decision maker.

Management accounting employs concepts from business economics to help you decide on future courses of action that can be justified on managerial grounds, so let's begin there.

Microeconomic concepts

Economic theory tries to explain everything from macro levels of universal market forces through to the micro levels of what goes on inside an organisation. Economic theory influences tactical and strategic decisions on pricing, performance management, marketing and future investment. MBA programmes often look at this topic from a perspective that assumes rational decisions are made by self-interested individuals who are motivated to maximise efficiency for economic return.

Here are five key microeconomic concepts that are basic to an understanding of finance.

1 Scarcity and utility

The basis for what most organisations do is **scarcity**. Simply put, a demand is created as soon as people perceive a shortage of something. When this happens, choices have to be made, and there is a close relationship between choice and scarcity. In the rational view of the individual (or the firm), scarcity plus enlightened self-interest lead to decisions based on available information. Organisations not only try to identify what is scarce (and in demand), they also see whether they can limit it, or add to it.

Utility is the level of expected satisfaction derived from a good or service. It might seem straightforward to expect that more of something provides greater satisfaction, but this is not so. Utility diminishes (the second sip is never as refreshing as the first).

2 Forms of competition

Perfect competition is a special (and theoretical) situation where there are enough buyers and sellers in a market – each with access to perfect information – that it is impossible for any single entity or party to influence the price, which is set in terms of the margin over the cost of production, not in terms of what others are charging. In perfect competition, demand drives down price only to a point where the threat of a new competitor is removed. A higher price would attract competition (i.e. it would be worth entering the market). A lower price is unprofitable. At this point it meets the optimal supply at a rate that produces normal profit, or what it takes to keep the business a going concern. Normal profit needs to be considered as a cost because the price set at this point is the minimum expectation of return. Perfect competition doesn't really exist, but its consideration guides just about all investment decisions and policy or law regulating markets, especially utilities.

The opposite of perfect competition is **monopoly**, another largely theoretical state where a dominant player supplies at a price of cost plus margin unrestricted by competition. Many markets operate as **oligopolies**, where there is limited competition between a few suppliers that are dominant in the market. These competing organisations tend to be of roughly the same size and will tend to act reactively and proactively in regard to competitors. The interdependence among players is what makes an oligopoly special and this drives strategic analysis and planning among *profit-maximising* firms. Oligopolies are often the subject of mathematical modelling of two theoretical players using *game theory*.

3 Costs and revenue

Revenue (or turnover) is defined by the effective demand in the market × price. **Costs** are dictated by the price paid for inputs (materials, labour and capital) and the efficiency in management of processes needed to transform them to outputs. A marginal cost is the change in total cost that results from the production of one extra unit. If costs for inputs are known, the total cost can be calculated. Microeconomics also recognises the opportunity cost of choosing one course of action over another.

4 Supply and demand curve

Supply and demand curves (see Figure 5.1) are lines plotted on a graph on axes of price (P) versus quantity (Q) and illustrate that:

▌ demand (D) is the ratio of how many or how much of a good or service a customer is willing to buy at a given price. The lower the price, the more that customers will want (in theory), though it matters also what alternatives are available and how much money you have to spend

▌ supply (S) is the ratio between the given price a supplier of a good or service must charge to cover costs and make a margin and the quantity that it can supply at that price. The higher the price, the more it can make or supply.

Demand curves slope downwards while supply curves slope up. At some point, these two theoretical lines meet in equilibrium where supply and demand are matched by what buyer and seller are willing to accept in price. When there is more demand for something than there is supply, a shortage results and, generally, the price will go up.

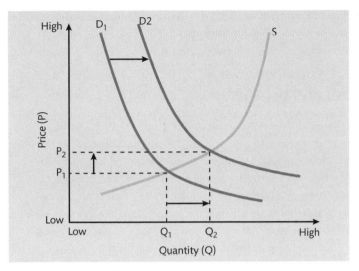

FIGURE 5.1 Supply–demand curve

Similarly, where there is an excess of supply, the price tends
to reduce. Getting the supply side of this equation correct is
crucial for many businesses and organisations, and this is
often the primary goal of operations managers. Elasticity is
the sensitivity between variables in a supply and demand
relationship. The ratio between a change in a price and the
demand for it is called the elasticity of demand. Inelastic is
if you put the price up (or down) and demand stays about
the same.

5 Economic profit (EP)

Economic profit is a way of measuring the effectiveness of
how resources are used. As a part of goal setting, evaluation
of performance, capital budgeting and valuation it can
be very important. Value is derived by subtracting cost
of capital from net operating profit over a given period.
EVA, or economic value added, is one way to show how
much wealth has been generated and is an alternative to

budgeted targets. It works only with accounting centres that are responsible for their own income, but can link several centres to track performance overall.

Costs and benefits

Decisions always need to be made about the best use of scarce resources. At some point the costs and benefits of your decisions will be assessed and measured beyond what was set out in a budget. One of the best ways of doing this is by calculating and comparing future marginal or additional costs and benefits resulting from a decision. Even if you have only one choice in mind, the comparison between that and what would happen if you just left things as they are can help.

For the purposes of most business or management decisions, the future is converted into a relationship between time and the value of money. It is no simple matter to measure every type of future benefit in money terms. Some of this is driven by an understanding of the concepts of demand and of supply, which will always incur a cost to make happen. There is a great deal of debate in accounting on the language of costs, but the most important principle to keep in mind is knowing which sorts are relevant to your decision making and which are not. The most basic division is between fixed costs (which don't change with increases or decreases in activity) and variable costs (which change in direct proportion to activity). Typically, tactical decision making involves using a set of assumptions to adjust capacity to meet demand and then modelling changes in variable costs to identify the break-even point (also known as cost-volume-profit analysis, or CVP). There is always an opportunity cost incurred, if only because the time used in one activity cannot then also be used to generate value in another.

> it is no simple matter to measure every
> type of future benefit in money terms

Another important aspect of this is whether an organisation is better off paying outside contractors or bringing work inside, often known as the make-or-buy decision, such as Morrisons outsourcing online and home delivery to Ocado (see case study above).

Future cash flows and net present value

Short-term decision analysis requires the following steps:

▌ Define the problem requiring a decision.

▌ Make a thorough list of alternative courses of action.

▌ Identify and discard alternatives that do not deserve closer analysis.

▌ Calculate the financial cost–benefit differences of the remaining choices.

▌ Weigh up the financial and non-financial factors to make a decision.

Longer term, options for growing or for development that do not rely on external sources of funding require an extension of managerial decision making beyond budgets. Finance now begins to resemble investment, and although the basic principles are the same as for short-term spending, there are several tools that a manager needs to know about to evaluate the different options open to them.

The most important consideration, bearing in mind the focus on value, is knowing the effect of any investment on future performance – whether replacing worn-out assets, cutting back on costs, funding internal expansion or reacting to external conditions. Most managers will not have direct responsibility for sourcing or appraising capital expenditure, but are fully involved in justifying, preparing and delivering such projects. It helps to know that the main financial criteria for justification of investment projects are that they:

▌ are in line with the objectives of the organisation

▌ will produce a return that exceeds the financing cost over their economic lifetime

▌ are the best choice financially among all those available, including their residual value at the end of the project.

Assuming that you can work out the future cash flows and predict the many variables that could affect this, how do you work out what's the best way to invest in a project?

The simplest method, payback period, compares the initial capital outlay for each option under consideration and calculates how long, in years, it will take to recover that original investment, and then how far into the expected economic life of the project this payback occurs. Payback is simple, but is unadjusted in that it ignores the time value of money (this is the fundamental idea in finance that money in the present is preferable to the same amount in the future). Techniques that factor in the value of the rate of return (or return on investment, ROI) over the whole economic life of the project need to adjust to this.

A commonly used technique to calculate the value of the various investment choices over a period of time longer than one year is net present value (NPV). If the present value of future benefits can be shown to exceed the present value of future costs, the project should be undertaken as it will add value to the organisation. Discounting is the process of finding the current value of future cash flows when they have been adjusted for future interest or inflation. What rate to discount at will usually be a given and is termed the cost of capital. Any project meeting this hurdle rate will, in theory, end up adding value.

Budgeting and budgets

An important sign of career progression is budgeting responsibility, so nearly all managers seek it. Actual budget preparation and appraisal can be the cause of much stress at work so it's worth looking at the distinction between the process and the product:

▌ **Budgeting** is a process to forecast the appropriate allocation, control and use of resources. It is often cultural, political and idiosyncratic (i.e. how one organisation goes about it is likely to be different from others). Budgeting cycles can be lengthy and expensive. For example, the Ford Motor Company spends in excess of $1 billion each year just on its budgeting process. For some, budgeting is an area of controversy because it is seen as being old-fashioned and out of touch with the fluid, project-based structures found in many companies.

▌ **A budget** is an approved plan that quantifies in monetary terms and over a fixed period an organisation's future activities. Because a budget predicts, it can be used as a control mechanism by prompting explanation of any difference or variance between the plan and the actual. Budgets may be incremental (new activities receive new funds), zero-based (each new round assumes activities are being done for the first time), rolling (on-going process of adding a new accounting period when the current one has expired) or flexible (designed to be adjusted to suit changes in activities).

ACTIVITIES FOR REFLECTIVE PRACTICE

1 Speak to your finance director. Ask them how they have changed their budgeting models since 2008.

2 How do they think the budgeting process could be improved in your organisation? How would any of those changes affect or involve you?

Budget variance and approval are day-to-day features which will be found in all organisations. The largest operating cost for many firms relates to people, but using budgets to manage staff performance is risky. Where this happens, managing variance produces short-term or self-interested thinking and becomes a stress on people.

Fluency in accounting should matter to you because it will help answer questions that go beyond how things are going compared with the plan. This is important because as a senior manager you will always need to answer four questions:

1 Do we have enough cash to pay the bills and remain viable?

2 How are we doing compared with our competitors?

3 Are we better or worse off than we were in the past?

4 What will our financial position be at a given time in the future?

> fluency in accounting should matter to you because it will help answer questions

1 Describe the relationship you have with your finance team during the budgeting cycle. Who is responsible for explaining any variance in your budget: you, your finance managers, or a combination?

2 What assumptions about budgeting have been used in your organisation?

To reach conclusions and understand the effective use of these and other accounting principles you must know something about using financial statements to produce financial ratios.

Financial accounting

The audience in financial accounting are people outside your organisation with an interest in how it is performing (whether you are creating value). Because companies with publically traded shares must publish their audited accounts in annual reports, we are able to examine their statements for the story behind the performance. Looking at the three financial statements from the 2012–13 accounts of Morrisons plc should provide a few clues to the decision making in the company around its tactical and strategic position in the market. Remember, the notes section of the annual report contains information to help you read the statements, as well as a lot of the company detail and background the consolidated numbers cannot show you.

Financial statements

All organisations must ensure access to cash, even when making a profit and especially when that business is new or has invested in non-current assets (e.g. equipment, vehicles and buildings that the organisation plans to own for more than one year). So first we need to understand the significance of the cash flow statement, not least because a lack of liquidity is the single most frequent reason businesses fail. See Table 5.1.

The cash flow statement consolidates income from three sets of activities: operating, investing and financing. The critical number on this statement is the £1,104 million that Morrisons generated from its operations in 2013, up from 2012. It is essential to generate this revenue inflow in order to invest in the business without relying on external sources of finance. If this number falls, then the company will be less able to finance its growth. You can see that the outflow was £1,008 million, which is what the company was able to invest in that year.

The cash flow statement is a common-sense record of actual (as opposed to booked) inflows and outflows of cash over a period, showing start and end cash balances. A cash flow forecast is the same, but for a future period. The advantage of this is that it enables management to adjust to future shortfalls in liquidity, either by sourcing funds temporarily to cover the cash shortfall or by speeding up the arrival of revenues and delaying outgoings from business activities.

The income statement, or profit and loss (P&L), covers the period of time between two balance sheets, but unlike the cash flow is not dependent on whether money has been received or spent yet (not only are 'profit' and 'cash' different concepts, but profit is multi-layered and potentially confusing as a comparable measure). Table 5.2 shows the Morrisons 2013 P&L.

The P&L is a retrospective (and statutory) annual income statement that shows the balance of revenue (turnover) less any direct cost of sales. This gives you the gross profit,

TABLE 5.1 Consolidated cash flow statement for Morrisons plc, 2012–13

	2013 (£ m)	2012 (£ m)
Cash flows from operating activities		
Cash generated from operations	**1,432**	1,264
Interest paid	**(85)**	(55)
Taxation paid	**(243)**	(281)
Net cash inflow from operating activities	**1,104**	928
Cash flows from investing activities		
Interest received	**3**	6
Investments	**–**	(31)
Proceeds from sale of property, plant and equipment	**5**	4
Purchase of property, plant and equipment, investment and software	**(846)**	(724)
Purchase of intangible assets	**(134)**	(72)
Cash outflow from acquisition of businesses	**(36)**	(74)
Net cash outflow from investing activities	**(1,008)**	(891)
Cash flows from financing activities		
Purchase of own shares	**(514)**	(368)
Purchase of treasury shares	**(65)**	–

▶

	2013 (£ m)	2012 (£ m)
Proceeds from exercise of share options	**42**	–
New borrowings	**843**	1,102
Repayment of borrowings	**(81)**	(486)
Dividends paid to equity shareholders	**(270)**	(301)
Net cash outflow from financing activities	**(45)**	(53)
Net increase/decrease in cash and cash equivalents	**51**	(16)
Cash and cash equivalents at start of period	**212**	228
Cash and cash equivalents at end of period	**263**	212

Source: **www.morrisons-corporate.com**

TABLE 5.2 Consolidated income statement for Morrisons plc, 2012–13

	2013 (£ m)	2012 (£ m)
Turnover	**18,116**	17,663
Cost of sales	**(16,910)**	(16,446)
Gross profit	**1,206**	1, 217
Other operating income	**80**	86
Administrative expenses	**(336)**	(329)
Losses arising on property transactions	**(1)**	(1)
Operating profit	**949**	973

	2013 (£ m)	2012 (£ m)
Finance costs	(75)	(47)
Finance income	5	21
Profit before taxation	879	947
Taxation	(232)	(257)
Profit for the period attributable to the owners of the company	647	690
Other comprehensive expense for the period, net of tax	(10)	(69)
Total comprehensive income for the period attributable to the owners of the company	637	690

Source: **www.morrisons-corporate.com**

from which all other expenses such as wages, overheads, dividends and due taxation are deducted, leaving the net profit (the infamous bottom line). The P&L is the most important measurement with input to strategy because it is what organisations use to measure themselves against their competition.

Morrisons turned over £18.11 billion in 2013, but the most important number here is the £637 million profit that is attributable to the owners. This represents a decrease from £690 million from the previous year (which was achieved on a lower turnover). On its own this does not indicate a strong performance (though look for some qualification in the report) and restricts what those in a governance position in the company can do because they must decide how much can be paid to shareholders in dividends.

what you see is a slice through the organisation on a given day

The balance sheet will show the good news, or the bad news, about what a business owns now compared with a year ago (see Table 5.3). What you see is a slice through the organisation on a given day. It's rather like a snapshot, or freeze frame, and – like many individuals who know they are going to be photographed – organisations will try to look their best on that date. This is certainly true for large companies that need to reassure investors or owners that they are creating value.

TABLE 5.3 Consolidated balance sheet for Morrisons plc, 2012–13

	2013 (£ m)	2012 (£ m)
Assets		
Non-current assets		
Goodwill and intangible assets	415	303
Property, plant and equipment	8,616	7,943
Investment property	123	259
Investments and other financial assets	31	32
	9,185	8,537
Current assets		
Stocks	781	759
Debtors	291	320
Cash and cash equivalents, other financial assets	270	243
	1,342	1,322

	2013 (£ m)	2012 (£ m)
Liabilities		
Current liabilities		
Creditors	**(2,130)**	(2,025)
Other financial liabilities	**(55)**	(115)
Current tax liabilities	**(149)**	(163)
	(2,334)	(2,303)
Non-current liabilities		
Other financial liabilities	**(2,396)**	(1,600)
Deferred tax liabilities	**(471)**	(464)
Net pension liabilities	**(20)**	(11)
Provisions	**(76)**	(84)
	(2,963)	(2,159)
Net assets	**5,230**	5,397
Shareholders' equity		
Called-up share capital	**235**	253
Share premium	**107**	107
Capital redemption reserve	**37**	19
Merger reserve	**2,578**	2,578
Retained earnings and hedging service	**2,273**	2,440
Total equity attributable to the owners of the company	**5,230**	5,397

Source: **www.morrisons-corporate.com**

The balance in a balance sheet is between what the company owns versus what it owes to third parties and shareholders. There are different ways of expressing this equation, for example Morrisons deducts liabilities from assets and then balances the result with what is owed to shareholders, but the basic formula is:

$$total\ assets = total\ liabilities$$

Assets are those resources owned by the business that can be represented in monetary terms and that are expected to be used in some way for economic benefit. Current assets include the working capital (anything 'liquid' or available in the short term to generate value), while fixed assets are those items that the organisation owns and that will have an expected economic life of more than one year.

On the other side, liabilities show where the organisation has a monetary obligation to others. This will include any loans outstanding as well as the capital invested by the shareholders, or reserves such as retained profits from past years.

As for Morrisons, if liquidated, it would be worth on paper £5,230 million because this is in effect the amount liable to the shareholders. You can see that this is less than the previous year, so arguably the company is not doing as well as it might have hoped. This is in line with the fall in profits in 2013.

Financial ratios

Ratios work by expressing one thing (e.g. profit) in relation to another (e.g. total assets) in order to provide useful **heuristic** information for decision making. It is not difficult to calculate ratios with the right data; the art lies in how you make sense of the results. But there are a great many key ratios, even at a high level, and too many to list in detail. The main categories are indicated below:

Profitability ratios: These look at earnings (profit) before interest and taxation as a percentage of total assets. Generally, the higher the ratio, the better the indicator of how much value the business is generating from its assets, but much depends on what is normal for that type of sector, or between similar competitors.

Liquidity, or working capital ratios: ('Can we pay our way?') It has already been mentioned that a business or organisation that has no cash available is not going to remain a going concern for very long. Liquidity ratios look at the way working capital cycles through a business.

Gearing, or leverage ratios: The two principal sources of financing a venture are shareholder equity and loans. The global recession that began in 2008 showed how access to short- and long-term loans is fundamental to businesses' growth and development. It is true that loans normally carry an interest obligation, but unlike dividends paid to shareholders, loans often benefit from the 'tax shield' and are deductible from tax. There is often an advantage in managing the relative amounts of debt from different sources. The relationship between debt and equity is called gearing.

Productivity ratios: An interesting use of financial ratios, though one that makes sense only in comparison with other factors, is to derive how much value is being provided by the human resource (nearly always an organisation's biggest cost).

Investor ratios: Finally, and frequently quoted for publicly traded companies, some specific ratios are used for investor decision making.

Ratios are something of a minefield for MBA students because they come alive through calculation and interpretation in a context. On the page they remain rather superficial. Because different organisations calculate and use them in different ways, it usually makes sense to get to know the ones that inform your industry, sector or company.

ACTIVITIES FOR REFLECTIVE PRACTICE

1 Visit **www.morrisons-corporate.com/2013/annualreport/ downloads/Default.aspx** to access the Morrisons 2013 annual accounts or **http://markets.ft.com/research/ Markets/Tearsheets/Summary?s=MRW:LSE** for the FT's snapshot. Take some time to review the financial statements and accompanying notes, paying attention to which ratios it uses to report its financial KPIs.

2 Speak with the finance team in your organisation. See which financial ratios are important to your business and ask how they are calculated.

Putting it together: it all adds up

Accounting is a universal language, but it is spoken in many different accents and dialects. Practice varies not just among companies but from sector to sector and country to country. The presence of external regulation and standardisation in accounting means that everyone has a platform for comparison to look at their performance, but an organisation's internal financial decision making will constantly evolve. The use of numbers, ratios and mathematics in managerial accounting doesn't mean there are no skills of interpretation or judgement required; on the contrary, deriving meaning from numbers is the craft of doing business.

The economic principles and use of accounting mentioned in this chapter have been about an organisation's past performance. In Chapter 8 we will revisit the finance link, but in terms of valuation and planning for the future.

Further reading

A classic text:	*Intelligent Investor: The definitive book on value investing – a book of practical counsel* by Benjamin Graham (2006), Collins Business. First published in 1949 and on Warren Buffett's list of top three books about finance.
Going deeper:	*Principles of Business Economics* by Joseph Nellis and David Parker (2nd Edition, 2006), Financial Times/ Prentice Hall. Contains everything you need to know.
Visit this:	'Beyond Budgeting Institute': **www.bbrt.org**. Dedicated to the sharing of best practice among organisations in planning and budgeting.

Note

1 **www.morrisons-corporate.com/**

QUESTIONS FOR REFLECTION

1 What does money mean to you?

2 Reflect on your career ambitions. What level of financial support or reward do you require to achieve your goals?

Strategic MBA thinking: how to manage the big picture

Strategy n. [ˈstrætɪdʒi/] a plan of action to achieve a
long-term goal, overall aim or desired end result

I n your organisation there are some things that are under
your control and other things that are not. We usually
think of those elements you can directly influence that
push you forward as strengths and those that hold you back
as weaknesses. What lies outside your control but could be
used to your advantage are *opportunities*, and what you can't
control but which could restrict you are *threats*. These are
the components of a SWOT analysis (see Figure P3.1). SWOT
came out of the failure of long-range corporate planning in
the US in the 1960s and 1970s and still typifies the sort of
framework applied to strategic decision and policy making
today.

The 'internal–external' dichotomy of a SWOT is an example
of a compelling idea in strategic thinking which we will

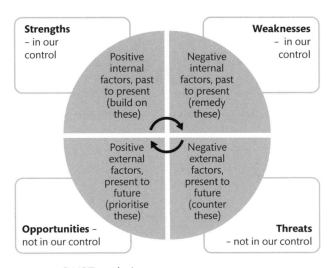

FIGURE P3.1 SWOT analysis

explore in this part. Strategic thinking is about making informed, intelligent choices from a set of considerations that extends beyond the boundaries, resources or culture of the organisation. Another way of looking at this is to say that strategy deals with what could be done in the future, and this future depends on the environment outside the organisation. But nothing in management is neat and tidy and strategic thinking requires managers to shift how they see the world.

Strategic thinking involves:

- understanding the delicate relationship between an organisation and its environment
- setting and communicating the goals and ensuring the survival of the organisation through value creation
- undertaking medium- to long-term planning and making a small number of (relatively) irreversible decisions
- keeping a cool head under pressure.

Strategic thinking in the early stages for any organisation is relatively simple. But as they grow and age, businesses develop more complex relationships with their internal and external environments. In particular they become more sophisticated regarding their customers. Or they should do. This requires a shift in management thinking beyond tactical decisions (though these remain important) to ones that deal with new and unpredictable variables. The cost of misjudgement may be high. In 2007, for example, the Royal Bank of Scotland under the leadership of Fred Goodwin purchased a large part of the Dutch bank ABN-AMRO. This was perfectly in line with RBS strategy – and very nearly precipitated a £46 billion government bailout to avoid the collapse of the world's largest banking group.[1]

There are four business areas associated with strategic thinking:

▌ marketing

▌ strategy

▌ corporate finance and governance

▌ global and international business.

We will see in turn how each of these is organised and how important it becomes to understand the language used to express ideas, concepts and theories at this level.

Note

1 www.theguardian.com/global/2011/dec/12/royal-bank-of-scotland-fsa-report

Marketing

The purpose of business is to create a customer.

Peter Drucker

In a nutshell

Marketing is about value as it is perceived by the customer. Every organisation has a customer because no organisation exists for long without demand for what it does. If demand changes, so must the organisation. In the eyes of your customer 'value' is not just about economics or functional needs, it is a connection to psychological desires and emotions, too.

In fact, some would even say that marketing is an all-encompassing philosophy of business. Marketing faculty at business schools tend to agree.

In this chapter you will:

▌ trace the history and development of marketing

▌ identify various marketing strategies available to organisations

▌ define brand and examine the importance of relationships with customers

▌ highlight how marketing happens between businesses

The value proposition

Marketing is the first MBA subject that explicitly moves between the internal and external environments of an organisation. Every organisation, whether multinational business, giant public institution, local charity or small start-up, will find marketing is the relevant perspective for setting levels of quality, service and price – the main components of the value proposition. This means that marketing is concerned first with identifying perceptions of value in the marketplace and then with the development, production and distribution of goods and services.

The tactical, practical and day-to-day business of marketing involves the implementation of projects and plans linked to the sale or advertising of what an organisation does. This is the domain of marketing as process and functional specialism. But the manager (and MBA student) should take a broader, strategic view that goes well beyond the marketing department.

Marketing is attuned to the way that the world – and the nature of competition – is changing. This makes it an exciting field of study with many stories and variants of application, but also a difficult one to define or keep completely up to date with.

ACTIVITIES FOR REFLECTIVE PRACTICE

1. Who is the person in charge of marketing in your organisation? What are the activities and responsibilities of this person? Ask them whether their marketing spend went up or down in the last five years. Ask for the reasoning behind their responses.

2. Who are your organisation's customers? What would you say is the value proposition of your company? (Think in terms of quality, service and price as perceived by your customers.

A (very) brief history of marketing

The Chartered Institute of Marketing gives its definition of marketing as:

the management process responsible for identifying, anticipating and satisfying customer requirements profitably.[1]

In 1960 a former executive of Pillsbury (a fast-moving consumer goods (FMCG) company), Robert Keith, summed up the development of marketing management in three ages:[2]

1. **The production era**: Following an explosion of mass production techniques (the Ford Model T assembly line is the archetypal example), the marketing task was to find ways to produce as much as possible as cheaply as possible. The focus was on profit from volume. Some have characterised this as the period before marketing, though this is not representative. Companies have engaged with their markets for centuries.

2. **The sales era; 'selling what we can make'**: In the boom years after the Second World War, there was a change. Supply began to outstrip demand and as competitors were able to apply the same production techniques, marketing shifted to finding innovative ways of persuading customers to buy the surplus of goods being produced.

3. **The marketing era; 'making what we can sell'**: From the 1960s on, companies switched to first understanding what the customer wants, then satisfying those needs (profitably). This may seem obvious, and some argue that it was like this all along, but it was not sophisticated, and big business had grown physically and psychologically away from the end-user. In this era, money was poured into finding new customers. The focus was now on market research to collect information about consumers

and competition, and processes for constant innovation for value creation.

Competitive advantage

The assumption of the marketing era is that others will try to be in the same space as you and will compete for market share by meeting the demands of your customers. This gives customers choice, which our economic system firmly believes to be a good thing, and has led to organisations becoming very, very interested in what strategies competitors are using. From this we get to the concept of competitive advantage, which is an idea proposed most firmly by Michael Porter in the 1980s that you should look at which resources and abilities within your organisation lead to performance at a *higher* level than your competitors (more about this in Chapter 7).[3] This has proved to be a powerful idea in shaping corporate behaviour.

Porter's view has found some opposition. First, there is the argument that marketing has only ever had one era – that of putting the customer first. Second, that this is a rather narrow model that does not match the complexity of the post-internet world. No one can argue that much has changed since the 1980s and 1990s and there's now a fourth marketing phase:

4 **The relationship era:** This wants the whole organisation to have a market orientation, where market research is aligned to the internal functions (including relationships with suppliers) and all levels of management are asked to embrace marketing principles across the organisation. There are two specific things that have helped define this new marketing:

   (a) a strategic focus on customer retention

   (b) the internet has led to a redefining of consumer power and a fragmenting of traditional marketing domains.

Digital marketing, in particular, has challenged many organisations to think again. In fact, social media has already had an enormous impact on marketers and digital marketing may one day need a whole chapter in its own right. Maintaining a consistent message is a much greater challenge in an age where users can generate their own content on, for example, YouTube or Facebook.

> social media has already had an enormous impact on marketers

Marketing in business schools has been dominated by one name: Philip Kotler. His book, *Marketing Management*, has been a mainstay on MBA courses for many years.[4] With an emphasis on the societal role of marketing, it is a comprehensive overview of a transformation from the marketing orientation to the relationship era. Kotler's work has highlighted the various ways of looking at marketing in terms of strategy.

Marketing strategies

A market orientation is meaningless without a coordinated strategy behind it. Michael Porter, again, has been influential in this regard by outlining three generic strategies for competitive advantage, each with roots in a different era in marketing:

1. **Cost leadership**: By minimising your costs you are able either to lower price or boost margin, so this is a strategy aimed at profitability. There are now links to Chapter 3 and how operations are organised, and to Chapter 5 and how financing is managed. There are strategic decisions required to have a lower cost base than your competitors because the scale needed to achieve this may require considerable capital investment.

2 Differentiation: This can be achieved only in the mind of the customer and it assumes access to the right information to know, or think they know. Differentiation may be real in the sense of features unique to your offering, or the result of careful promotion and branding.

3 Focus: This means finding a niche and concentrating only on that (at least to begin with). The niche may be a particular need or segment, and the growth of the internet has made it possible to reach previously difficult-to-get-to areas.

ACTIVITIES FOR REFLECTIVE PRACTICE

1 Is the marketer's definition of value in conflict with the finance manager's (Chapter 5)? Are these aligned with the view of the CEO (Chapter 1)? What about the shareholder?

2 Economic value can be derived either from the production end (costs) or the consumption end (price) of the value chain. At which end of the spectrum does your organisation place most of its energy?

Porter's influence is slowly fading, partly because the business world he was describing has become more fragmented. Let's examine how someone else has perceived this. The six markets framework was devised by Adrian Payne at Cranfield University and is an example of an analytical tool for market orientation (see Figure 6.1). Keeping the 'classic' customer in the centre of things, it extends marketing to other domains, such as suppliers (this is sometimes called reverse marketing), recruiters of talent, and the potential contained in referrals from existing customers and agents or other intermediaries. An analysis is then made of any gaps or changes between past, current and future focus in the organisation.

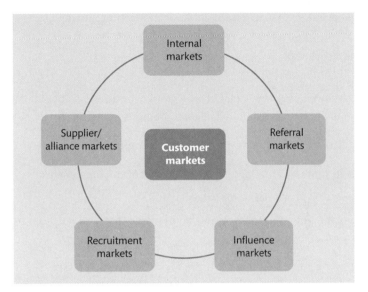

FIGURE 6.1 Six markets model
Source: Payne, A., Ballantyne, D. and Christopher, M. (2005) 'A stakeholder approach to relationship marketing strategy: The development and use of the "six markets' model'", *European Journal of Marketing*, 39(7/8): 855–871. Reproduced with permission of Emerald Group Publishing Ltd.

This still leaves plenty of open questions, and opportunities. What is the market definition of what you do? Is it better to lead or follow others in the market? What are the things under the control of the organisation and what are the things outside (remember SWOT)? What are you doing with the direct contact you now have with your customers?

Segmentation, targeting and positioning

Limited resources and competitors in the same space mean organisations have to identify groups of customers with similar needs and similar expectations of a value proposition. This is called segmentation, but there are many ways of slicing up a potential market. Below are a few examples:

- **geographic**: by particular region or district, urban versus rural, or populations living in different climates
- **demographic**: by gender, age group, income bracket, educational level
- **psychographic**: by social class, social aspirations, values, behaviours, lifestyle choices and attitudes to value.

An attractive segment for a company is one that:

- is in line with the long-term objectives of the organisation
- is within reach using resources available
- has the potential to grow and be of a size that will sustain a profitable return.

Thorough identification of all the segments in the market will allow selection of those worth targeting. Targeting may also be sub-divided into various decisions between differentiation and concentration within the segment. The ultimate goal for an organisation is to target customers one to one, and in some markets this sort of bespoke service is possible. Most companies, however, need to think carefully about the third step, positioning, where a detailed understanding of emotion, attitude and beliefs as drivers of value perception becomes crucial. Positioning statements connect the resources in an organisation to the segment it is targeting. They are expressions of how you want to be seen through the eyes of your customers. For example, Austrian energy drink company Red Bull[5] has employed 'wings' as a word and theme in its advertising for more than 25 years. This is a tactical and, by now, strategic choice.

> the ultimate goal for an organisation is to target customers one to one

The link to the tactical: from the four to the seven Ps

The four Ps of marketing developed by E. Jerome McCarthy in the 1960s have now attained seminal status in marketing management.[6] For the record, they are:

▌ **Product**: Different eras have developed the idea of the product from 'what we make' to 'what needs making'. In theory, this is a constantly shifting issue and few organisations can keep on making the same thing without adjustments, innovation or reinvention. The customer has to be able to see the value for them of what your company does and this is the core benefit.

▌ **Price**: For you, price is revenue, not cost (all other marketing Ps entail cost). To your customer your price is a cost of their time, effort or money. A market orientation equates the value of a thing with what the customer is willing to pay for it. There are many considerations behind what price to set and profit is only one of them. Price, for example, may also establish your value position vis à vis your competitors. How you identify the features of your product as benefits for your customers may also be important.

▌ **Place**: This used to be a very obvious matter of naming channels and locations for purchase. Availability in an increasingly interconnected and online world, even for tangible goods and traditional services, is more complex. The logistics of delivering and displaying your offering are critical to your customer's perception of value to them, and if they see a better alternative, unless you have a strong brand loyalty they will move.

▌ **Promotion**: Communication with your customers (which, by the way, is also communication with your competitors) includes branding, advertising, public relations and gaining the attention of others with a consistent message. Increasingly, these channels are now set up as a form of two-way communication and collection of market data.

Academics and thinkers find it hard to resist alliteration, and the original four have since been expanded to reflect the importance in globalised economies of service industries:

▌**People**: Chapter 4 highlighted the crucial role that human resources play in the success of any organisation, and contact points with customers will almost certainly include a personal element (or will need one when things don't go well). By including people in the marketing mix, you are saying that training, attitude and consistent service or support are as important as any other element.

▌**Process**: Many processes are not designed with the customer in mind, so this P is often overlooked. It is added in recognition that the customer experience of any process that delivers your offering is crucial to retention and reputation. Having to wait, not being kept informed and not being treated with respect – all can have a devastating effect on the bottom line (in Chapter 11 we look at this again as reputation).

▌**Physical evidence**: Making the intangible service feel more tangible is incredibly important for marketers. In some ways this relates to 'place', above, but extends to include, for example, word-of-mouth testimonials of others, awards and certificates of excellence, and pre-purchase access to others who are already customers.

This palette in the marketing mix is an attractive framework to organise basic ideas, but is under severe pressure when you try to use it to keep up with the fragmented and rapidly changing consumer environment. How easily can you apply these to Google, iTunes or Facebook without presenting their *business models* as simplistic, or – in theory – wrong?

The shift from product to brand

The placement of a financial value of a company's brand (often found in financial statements) is probably a double-edged sword for marketing. On the one hand it raises the status and profile of the marketing function and enables budget allocation of funds to marketing activities, but on the other it remains very difficult to know the effect of marketing spend on the bottom line. In a business or organisation with few physical assets, value is also derived from the perceived reputation, of which the brand is usually the major component. The Coca-Cola Company owns relatively few tangible assets (other than production of the all-important concentrate) and it is estimated that at least 50 per cent of its market capitalisation is derived just from the premium of the brand name and bottling contracts. For McDonald's, the comparable figure is 70 per cent.[7]

I can recall attending a conference in Budapest in the mid-1990s, where I watched the CEO of Saatchi and Saatchi worldwide, Kevin Roberts, deliver a presentation about our relationship with brands. He traced a development from a commodity to a product, and from a product to a brand, and then proposed an idea beyond a brand: the lovemark. This is a product or provider that delivers beyond your expectations and somehow creates a connection to heart as well as head.

ACTIVITIES FOR REFLECTIVE PRACTICE

1 What are some of your favourite brands? What do those choices say about you?

2 How do you define your 'personal brand'? What are you most known for where you work?

Brands present us with choices. We like to believe these are individual, but they also communicate something about us to others. Take a look at what a major brewing company has to say on this subject in the case study.

The brand strategy of Belgian brewer Anheuser-Busch

The extract below is from the company's 2013 annual report and captures how Anheuser-Busch see its value proposition to its customers. Notice how the alignment includes the intentions of those working in the company.

> When people get together over a beer, they're not simply sharing a favorite beverage. They're sharing moments, adventures, traditions, inspirations, opportunities and much more – the ingredients that make lasting friendships. At Anheuser-Busch InBev, we're equally passionate about brewing beer and brewing friendships. We pour ourselves into everything we do: our work, our connections with consumers, our engagement with employees, and our commitment to create a Better World. And that's why, across the globe, you'll find our beers wherever friendships are shared and great moments are savored.[8]

The company goes on to expand on the targeting strategy for the 200 brands in its portfolio (which includes Budweiser, Stella Artois and Corona):

> At Anheuser-Busch InBev, our brands are the foundation of the company, the cornerstone of our relationships with consumers, and the key to our long-term success.

Focus Brands

> We know focus works. This is why we have rigorously reinforced our focus brands strategy. Focus brands are those in which we invest most of our marketing money,

and to which we dedicate the greatest proportion of our share of mind. With a portfolio of well over 200 brands, we are prioritizing a small group with greater growth potential within each relevant consumer segment. These focus brands include our three global brands, key multi-country brands, and 'local jewels'.

Values Based Brands

All of our brands must have clearly defined and consistently communicated values, making them 'Values Based Brands'. The process of defining these values is a key discipline for all marketing activities in our business and is proving particularly powerful in renovating and innovating our premium brands around the real and changing habits and preferences of consumers.[9]

Source: Anheuser-Busch InBev

ACTIVITIES FOR REFLECTIVE PRACTICE

1. Recently, Anheuser-Busch has started to measure ROI on its digital marketing strategy. Read this short article about its branding online and try to identify the pros and cons the company faces.[10]

2. What is your organisation doing about the use of social media platforms in its marketing and branding?

The product life cycle

A product, according to Philip Kotler, is 'anything that can be offered to a market to satisfy a want or need'.[11] The term includes not just tangible goods but services, too. An experience, a cause, a person or even an idea, all these are potentially viable offerings as long as there is a market for them. Traditionally the focus in marketing has been on how to present features of an offering in terms of benefits for a customer. Perceptions of benefits and the value they present change over time, something that the product life cycle expresses (see Figure 6.2). Popularity grows, peaks and then eventually wanes. In fact, a product is defined by this time-based phenomenon of shifting tastes and demand.

> perceptions of benefits and the value they present change over time

A successful product has phases. From development and introduction to market, to sales growth and then a plateau of maturity, before eventual decline. This is the background to many of the functional areas we looked at in Part Two (planning for delivery of a good or service, management of cash flows and investment, and proper management of the people involved). For those involved in marketing, this cycle is also a guide for where and what to do tactically and strategically for the replacement or extension of products. Communication around this concept is therefore a two-way necessity between all departments in an organisation.

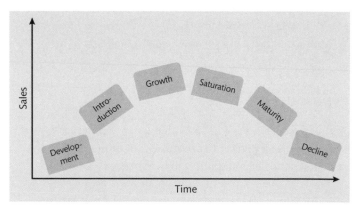

FIGURE 6.2 The product life cycle model

1. Describe the features of one or more of the brands in the organisation you work for (or the branding of your organisation, if this is more appropriate).

2. Select one product or service in your organisation and try to establish in your own mind where on the life cycle model it currently is. What options are there for managing it? Then canvas opinions of others in different functional areas. If appropriate, check this with senior management.

Relationship marketing: customer retention

The scope of modern marketing is being extended through a combination of the internet and the pressure on organisations to grow by maintaining profitable margins. Gaining customers is one thing, but retaining them is now seen as the best route to margin and the best way to do that is through what is known as relationship marketing (RM).

Aside from customer retention, RM has the following characteristics:

- Quality is a concern for everyone (highlighted already in Chapter 3 but now driven by feedback from the end-user).
- Standards of service in points of contact with the customer, measured against expectation and against competitors.
- A long-term and personal relationship with the customer, and attempt at alignment with their values.
- Measurable returns in terms of net present value (highlighted in Chapter 5) in excess of transactional marketing tactics.

> even when a company is fully
> committed to CRM, it's not easy to get
> right

Customer relationship marketing (CRM) is a further refinement of this, often in the form of investment in IT and database management. CRM is supposed to be under the control of general management rather than just a feature of the marketing department. However, the disadvantage of it being under general control is that it tends to monetise the relationship with the customer. Short time horizons in many companies make the customer relationship one of short-term targets in order to achieve returns on any investment. Long-term benefits may be more important but are harder to show on paper. Even when a company is fully committed to CRM, it's not easy to get right. For example, making bold customer care promises that are then not kept is very destructive, and even a genuine wish to engage with the customer can easily be translated into a kind of 'stalking' (e.g. follow-up surveys after every transaction).

Business-to-business marketing (B2B)

Millions of businesses are suppliers to other businesses, and of course millions more are themselves customers for innumerable products and services from other suppliers. It's likely that many of you reading this book are employed in organisations that rely – in one way or another – on relationships and transactions with other organisations. Business-to-business marketing shares many similarities with business-to-consumer (B2C), but there are some important differences. In B2B:

▌ Buyer behaviour is reportedly driven more by logic than by emotion, though values are often key to setting the boundaries for what is and what is not acceptable (Chapter

11 will discuss some of these issues). B2B may involve a buy decision that involves many individuals (some of whom may, of course, be people with emotions!).

▌ Both parties need to pay attention to the value propositions of the other. Aligning yourself to meeting the needs of your customer's customer creates a strong value proposition in its own right.

▌ The cost of a sale is generally much higher than in B2C and so is the complexity of the buyer–seller relationship.

Players in a supply chain tend to be conservative and they prefer more permanent relationships with each other (unless they find reasons not to). For a corporation, relationships with end-users are much harder to fix. In contrast, consumers face less risk and have more choice in their purchases and will easily switch (unless they find reasons not to).

ACTIVITIES FOR REFLECTIVE PRACTICE

1 Who manages the relationships with suppliers to your organisation? If you can, speak with them about how they see the B2B marketing process.

2 What percentage of your organisation's annual turnover is spent on marketing? How would you go about benchmarking this?

Putting it together: not a question of life or death – marketing is much more important than that

Marketing is tied closely to behaviour because it's what organisations do, as perceived by their customers. Customers care about the 'ends', which are the products they experience, but increasingly they care also about the 'means', or the practices used to make and deliver those products. It's easy to see how trust could be built or destroyed by refusal to act ethically and in line with the law or with generally accepted norms. There is plenty of room for grey areas, though. All the 7Ps of marketing have ethical dimensions. For example, where does a company draw the line between a strategy of price differentiation (e.g. creating opportunities for consumers to pay a lower price for the same product) and price discrimination (e.g. some customers having no choice but to pay a different price)?

When you define value exclusively as 'what the customer says it is', you risk taking a viewpoint that ignores other stakeholders, not least the shareholders, founders or owners of the business. Marketing is an exciting, engaging activity, but it is not only tactical. It is the outward, creative expression of strategic creativity. For middle and senior managers, there are still plenty of unanswered questions:

1. **Tactical**: as a function of business, what direction will marketing take next? What innovations to practice will emerge, especially in the digital environment? How can it be managed in such a dynamic environment?

2. **Strategic**: as a business philosophy, is marketing an end or a means to a different end? What will be the role of marketing in the bigger picture of management?

There is little evidence of a major shift in our thinking about marketing. Change seems to be more incremental than revolutionary, and for all its creativity, marketing is following, not leading, the strategic discussion. The critic argues that we are still looking for tactical ways to reinvent the wheel, and strategic ways of making that wheel bigger. But it's still a wheel. It usually takes some kind of trauma to kick-start a period of deep reflection and re-evaluation (similar to an aspect of personal development in Chapter 2).

The term marketing – when used strategically as a whole-business philosophy – includes not only the relationships with customers but that with competitors, too. Without customers you have no business. Without competitors you have no identity. Between these is now, as there has always been, a whole range of influencers (one of the six in the six markets framework). Perhaps it is this rich set of interactions that makes marketing so fluid and unpredictable.

Further reading

A classic text:	*Marketing Management* by Philip Kotler *et al.* (2nd Edition, 2012), Pearson. A hefty book with a hefty price tag, but not much escapes its breadth of content.
Going deeper:	*Purple Cow: Transform your business by being remarkable* by Seth Godin (2010), Portfolio.
	A Very Short, Fairly Interesting and Reasonably Cheap Book About Studying Marketing by Jim Blythe (2006), Sage Books. A personal and readable account by an experienced author in marketing.
Watch these:	'David Ogilvy: the essentials', a short montage of clips about advertising legend David Ogilvy. Get some big ideas! http://youtu.be/yj9rokSeack
	'The most boring ad ever made?' Leica challenges you to watch 45 minutes of careful polishing, and makes its point about the brand: http://youtu.be/PpSMW5H7FPQ

Notes

1 www.cim.co.uk/files/7ps.pdf

2 Keith, R.J. (1960) 'The marketing revolution', *Journal of Marketing*, 24(3): 35–38.

3 Porter, M.E. (2004) *Competitive Advantage*, New Edition, Free Press.

4 Kotler, P., Lane, K., Brady, M., Goodman, M. and Hansen, T. (2012) *Marketing Management*, 2nd Edition, Pearson.

5 http://energydrink.redbull.com/commercial#video/2470339735001

6 McCarthy, J.E. (1960) *Basic Marketing: A managerial approach*, Richard D. Irwin.

7 www.hrexaminer.com/the-fair-market-value-of-employees/

8 www.ab-inbev.com/go/media/annual_report_2013, Anheuser-Busch InBev. Extract reproduced with permission.

9 http://www.ab-inbev.com/go/brands/brand_strategy, Anheuser-Busch InBev. Extract reproduced with permission.

10 http://digiday.com/brands/inside-anheuser-buschs-digital-strategy/

11 Kotler, P. *et al.* (2012) *Marketing Management*, European Edition, Pearson, p. 574.

QUESTIONS FOR REFLECTION

1 As a manager, have you ever had to do something you didn't want to do? How were you persuaded? How did you cope?

2 Have you ever made someone at work undertake a task they didn't want to do? How did you persuade them? How did they cope?

Strategy

7

All men can see these tactics whereby I conquer, but what none can see is the strategy out of which victory is evolved.

Sun Tzu

In a nutshell

Is a strategy something you have, or something that you do? Should a strategy be synonymous with the purpose of business? Or is it just a means to an end? How you connect strategy to other subject areas will depend on how you answer such big questions. Marketing and international business, for example, both rely on a strategic overlap, and any aspect of financial management with capital expenditure or long-term financial interests of the owners is strategic. In fact, what isn't strategic, you could ask. No wonder that people love talking and writing about it. In business schools, it sometimes seems that students and faculty rarely talk of anything else.

People have had something to say about strategy for millennia, and for much longer than we have used the word in management and business. This chapter acknowledges that past but will focus, too, on current thinking in strategic decision making.

In this chapter you will:

▌ differentiate between the main approaches to strategy

▌ examine the external and internal strategic environments

▌ define competitive advantage

▌ engage with strategic planning

'Old school' strategy

Strategy, said Peter Drucker, is our answer to the questions 'What is our business, what should it be, what will it be?'[1] It would be fair to say that Drucker saw strategy as the cement between the building blocks of an organisation.

Invariably on an MBA you are told three things about strategy:

1 It is a concept with roots in (ancient and modern) military campaigns and is about victory over defeat. Many people therefore see 'winning' in business as synonymous with strategic thinking. With this comes the idea that the purpose of strategy is to ensure the continued survival of the firm, business or organisation.

2 It ensures the long-term viability of an organisation through sustainable competitive advantage. When the individual firm is the unit of survival, strategy's function is to find and then protect from competitors the sources of value creation. Strategy needs to control the internal and then exploit external resources of what is defined as its unique competing space.

3 It is the capstone subject, the one that binds all other topics in management under one unifying principle. It is also synonymous with a more sophisticated level of MBA thinking than the tactical.

The problem of the unique competing space

So, strategy is about winning in the long term and is the culmination of the journey in management. However, there are criticisms of this view which we also need to explore. On an MBA, strategy generally centres itself on the competitive position of the organisation in what is sometimes called its unique competing space. This begins with a search to understand why there is an organisation in the first place, followed by analysis of the boundary between purpose and environment (the external and internal bases of competitiveness).

The problem here is if we speak of an ever-changing unique competing space as if the organisation would still exist without it. The organisation implies the competing space just as much as the space implies the organisation. You couldn't have one without the other. There are two consequences:

1. If strategy wants to be transformational, then analysis must acknowledge that the unit of survival is never a single organisation but the organisation plus its environment. No strategy will be truly transformational and sustainable otherwise.

2. If strategy equalled only the analysis, your plans would be left gathering dust on the shelves. Strategy without action is meaningless. Only when we implement do we find anything out.

Not for the first time in the book, the crucial link between strategic sense making or planning and results in the bottom line is you – the middle manager. Your role is always strategic.

The structure of strategy

It might surprise you to learn that strategy is a relative
newcomer as a core component of business administration.
During and after the Second World War interest grew in
how an organisation could sustain itself and in particular
how economies could plan to rebuild themselves, and
strategy as its own subject became an explicit part of the
MBA curriculum from the late 1950s onwards, mainly
in the United States. Originally, it was about rational
decision making based on scenario planning, and the use of
quantifiable techniques. This was applied to the organisation
in an era of support for management science, but also one
with a new interest in the psychology of human relations,
especially in Europe.

On its own a strategy is just an expression of a direction. It
needs to be translated from lofty goals and objectives that
then have to be implemented. The context for strategy is
the same as the purpose of a business. Purpose is usually
verbalised in mission statements (present-tense expressions
of why the organisation exists) and vision statements (future-
focused pictures of the goals, ethics, beliefs and values).

> the context for strategy is the same as
> the purpose of a business

Here is how Procter and Gamble expresses it:

Our Purpose

We will provide branded products and services of superior quality and value that improve the lives of the world's consumers, now and for generations to come. As a result, consumers will reward us with leadership sales, profit and value creation, allowing our people, our shareholders and the communities in which we live and work to prosper.[2]

Plenty of vision and aspiration, but there is a danger that this view of strategy can feel very top-down and remote from the experience elsewhere in the organisation. An alternative view of strategy is that it must emerge as the organisation grows, from both the top and the bottom up.

Most strategists agree that competition is a central characteristic of any free market economy. The orthodox view is that the key to a successful business is the development of a profitable (or sustainable, if not-for-profit) business model that identifies customers, analyses competitive advantage, anticipates competitor actions and looks for novelty and innovation to maintain this advantage. Michael Porter was not the first to write about it, but his book *Competitive Strategy* set the tone for other theorists and practitioners.[3] Porter said that the components of strategic analysis are a firm's:

▌ **external environment**: the opportunities and threats presented by competitors, markets, macroeconomics

▌ **internal environment**: the strengths and weaknesses inherent in an organisation's resources, skills and microeconomics.

In Porter's models these are defined and analysed independently, then combined to bring together all the resources required to differentiate yourself in the eyes of your customers. In contrast, Henry Mintzberg sees strategy less as orderly structure and planning and more as 'a pattern in a stream of decisions'.[4] Mintzberg developed a view of strategy as what emerges when your plan meets reality, in the here and now. Crucially, this also makes middle management the vital link in the value chain because what happens there is what will make the difference for your ability to achieve a strategy. Porter essentially restricts strategy to senior management, who analyse what should be happening. Porter's model also says the firm can and should influence its environment, whereas success in Mintzberg's view comes from a judicious combination of i) the use of resources at hand and ii) the speed of innovation.

Internal vs. external is a central idea in strategic analysis, as we saw with the SWOT analysis, so let's stick with the approach and look at each in turn.

The external competitive environment

Making sense of the world outside the organisation is one of the main responsibilities of senior management. There are few specific principles to rely on for this so it means the best way to begin is with broad frameworks. The most all-encompassing of these are found in the six categories known as PESTEL:

Political: Governments pass laws, set and collect taxes, influence employment policies and intervene in the economy. Where this affects your organisation, you will need to understand how these laws are created and implemented. Transnational groupings such as the EU bring an even wider backdrop of stability (or instability) to this context.

Economic: These are the macro factors that are the boundaries of economic growth, such as interest rates, wage rates, exchange rates, etc. In an interconnected economy almost every organisation is affected by this aspect.

Social: Many cultural norms also influence the business environment, such as population demographics and societal divisions. Public opinion can make or break an organisation's strategy. Shifts in wealth, neglect of human rights, imbalances in gender equality and access to education are all examples of social factors.

Technological: The advances in knowledge brought about by science, the advances in communication enabled by the internet and computational power of computing are all examples of this.

Environmental: This includes concerns over climate change, exploration and exploitation of the environment for natural resources, agriculture and the effects of continued urbanisation globally, and the creation and treatment of waste.

Legal: This covers the laws and regulatory environment, including the level of enforcement and exploitation of loopholes in different parts of the world.

PESTEL is used to identify which external factors have the most impact on internal conditions, so a more detailed analysis at the organisational level would follow. It is an inclusive checklist that addresses the question: 'What is the business environment like?' It does not answer the follow-up question: 'Is this a good environment for us?'

For this, we may turn again to Porter. The key model of a firm's competitive environment is his Five Forces model, first presented in a landmark 1979 *Harvard Business Review* article as a reaction to what he saw as the over-simplified format of the SWOT.[5] Five Forces has attracted its critics in recent years but is still widely used. The big idea is that the attractiveness (i.e. profitability) of an industry or sector is the interplay of five factors and you analyse whether the influence on your organisation of each is high, medium or low:

▊ **Rivalry between firms**: the central idea. Competition for market share will be fierce if competitors are well balanced or if consumers can easily switch.

▊ **Threat of new entrants**: you are vulnerable if there are no barriers to entry to your industry. New rivals can easily force your margins down as you compete for customers.

▊ **Bargaining power of buyers**: this is high if your customers can put pressure on you, are sensitive to price, or if your structure has high fixed costs and your margins are low.

▊ **Threat of substitutes**: this is high if customers can easily (i.e. cheaply) meet a need or a want in another way. This is why Coca-Cola owns so many other ways of satisfying your thirst.

▊ **Bargaining power of suppliers**: this is high if you rely on only certain suppliers, or those suppliers would have a low cost to switch away from you (the inclusion of suppliers and buyers links to Porter's value and supply chain concepts mentioned earlier).

Porter's model has been 'top of the pops' for a long time and is worth applying because it forces you to ask some good questions about your business model. Its limitation is that it assumes possession of perfect information and that the context is relatively stable. Complexities in the contexts surrounding each of the Five Forces are not reflected in the analysis and there has been little empirical evidence that any industry or sector actually conforms to this model. Nor does it easily explain alliances and cooperative behaviours among players in a market, which are commonplace.

> Porter's model has been 'top of the pops' for a long time

Trader Media drives from print to digital

How we sell and buy used and new cars has been transformed in recent years. This excerpt from the *Financial Times* highlights the background and the shift in strategic direction of Auto Trader, the UK's largest automotive classified advertiser:

> Auto Trader attracts about seven out of every 10 page views on all UK car classified sites. At any one time, it has about 380,000 car listings in the UK. And last month it had 3.5m unique users on its mobile site, up from 2.2m a year before. The company operates primarily in the UK with subsidiary operations in Ireland and South Africa, making most of its money selling classified advertising to car dealers – in print but mostly online and via mobile. Total revenues were £257.2m for the year to the end of March last year, and this year the company's earnings before interest, tax, depreciation and amortisation from its digital operations alone are expected to be about £130m. In 2002 the company ran an overall ebitda loss of £10m.
>
> These numbers are impressive. But they are particularly so given what is happening to the wider economy, where the upgrade cycle for car owners has edged closer to four years away from a previous average of about three years, and at its core print title *Auto Trader* where readership is halving every year. In its heyday the classifieds car magazine, with a weekly circulation of more than 300,000, was the bible for anyone looking to buy or sell a second-hand car in the UK. Today its print run stands at only 40,000. Indeed, the future of its flagship print title is now in doubt, says Zillah Byng-Maddick, Trader Media's chief executive.
>
> The company has successfully navigated these headwinds by cutting costs – in less than 10 years the company's UK

▶

workforce has shrunk from about 3,600 to about 1,200 – and by closely following consumer trends. And that has meant being digital. The success of its website autotrader. co.uk has not only given the company deep insight into the online second-hand car market; it can prove, for example, that nine photos are the optimum number of images to secure a car sale. It has also given it reams of data, enabling it to expand into new business areas, such as running websites for car dealers. 'The richness of data we collect enables us to create new products we couldn't foresee when we first shifted to digital,' says Ms Byng-Maddick, who stepped up from chief financial officer to take over as CEO from John King last year.

This is a rich case for strategists. Is Auto Trader's new direction a result of internal or external logic? It is following the market and consumer behaviour while also reacting to the threat of competitors taking market share and substitute channels which may be new entrants. The move is a seismic change of culture because from print to digital has meant shedding old jobs and hiring in new skills. The culture change involves modernising suppliers (car dealers), too, not just customers. All sorts of new revenue opportunities from an expertise in mobile technology may also present themselves.

The internal competitive environment

The external approach scans the world for its nature and its opportunities. You start with what you find. The internal approach to strategy starts with what you know you have got and with the things you know you can do best. The resource-based view (RBV) measures your company's competitive advantage in terms of the:

- **intangible** asset of human capital (knowledge management, and the talents, skills and experience of people) and their social capital (the networks that those people have)
- **tangible** assets of equipment, machinery, reputation, funding and so on.

To form an advantage, however, these resources need to be difficult for your competitors to imitate. They must also provide access to important market segments and contribute to the value proposition.

ACTIVITIES FOR REFLECTIVE PRACTICE

1 What does your organisation have that others near you in your competing space could not easily imitate?

2 What does your closest competitor or comparison organisation have that would be difficult for you to copy?

The internal view is an argument to make strategy based on your core competencies. We looked at competencies for individuals in Chapter 2, but they have easily been applied to organisations as well. C.K. Prahalad and Gary Hamel were the main champions of this 'inside-to-outside' approach in the 1990s.[6] They proposed combining people skills with technology to foresee what value might look like in the future. However, for them the exercise is not just a list of what you're good at, it is more a willingness to view all qualities of the business as fluid, receptive to change and capable of exploiting future opportunities. Examples of companies that have been agile in reinventing themselves include Nokia (rubber to mobile phones), IBM (from adding machines, to mainframes, to clone PCs, to consulting and IT) and India's Wipro (vegetable products to IT consulting).

Many organisations with a large enough critical mass can reinvent themselves in subtle ways. Xerox, for instance, now sells more services than copiers, while Netflix recovered from a collapse of sales in rental DVDs to re-emerge in online streaming of content, including its own productions. Enron's rise and very public fall was an unethical form of reinvention, an example of the systemic dangers of hubris and unsustainable greed disguised behind a veneer of favourable company HR policies. The economy is clearly an ecosystem where many more companies will fail than survive, even those with (on paper) all the right ingredients.

Assessing competitive advantage

An organisation's competencies are difficult to define, except perhaps in hindsight. Even if strategy fortune-telling were true, competencies can walk out of your organisation before the much planned-for opportunity arrives. The future is by definition unpredictable and despite the number of consultants out there, no one has yet written the definitive book of rules on how to maintain a truly sustainable competitive advantage.

> an organisation's competencies are difficult to define, except perhaps in hindsight

I've mentioned competitive advantage several times now. On a good MBA you always define your terms, so what exactly does the phrase mean? First, there can be no advantage without disadvantage, so this is fundamentally a comparison against others (a ratio, in fact). Second, organisations need to be viable to sustain themselves, so this must be tied very closely to cash flow where the advantage is achieved ultimately through either profit margins or control of costs. Is this what competitive advantage boils down to? It may be a very relevant question to ask. Scottish economist John Kay's 1993 model for distinctive capabilities lists three sources of competitive advantage.[7] Each is quite difficult to achieve and none fits neatly into any formula or recipe:

▌ **Architecture**: the network of relationships and routines that sustains the identity of the organisation over time. This links us to many other themes in *The Every Day MBA*, such as organisational culture and supply chain management. Architecture includes the strategic managing of knowledge and flows of information. Any such aspect you have but that is unavailable to others constitutes a real advantage because it is systemic and hard to imitate.

▌ **Reputation**: the whole point of pursuing quality is to establish in the mind of your customers that it is worthwhile maintaining their relationship with you. Traditionally, this loyalty was seen as important only for products experienced over the long term and used regularly. This is changing and I would argue that it is important in every case (see Chapter 11). This long-term relationship between buyer and seller seeks an equitable balance of exchange. Customers must feel they are receiving value and will be happy to pay for this if they are sure they are respected, and buyers must feel they are not being forced to undersell what they do. Reputation involves the delicate give and take of trust ('trust us, we know what we're doing') and once gained is the second source of real advantage.

▌ **Innovation**: the third distinctive capability is the most difficult to turn into a competitive advantage. This may be because of the uncertainties of return on future investments (which we looked at in Chapter 5) or because there are few recipes for introducing new offerings ahead of competitors. If you can do this, perhaps through innovative research and development (R&D), it may well give you an edge. Innovation, though, carries risk. Being the first mover in a market is sometimes a critical element for strategy (as in the pharmaceutical sector), but it doesn't always pay off.

Kay's thinking borrowed from game theory, which did not capture the unpredictable nature of open systems such as consumer markets or, ultimately, the globalised economy. He has since refined and added to his ideas and suggests that strategic success is often oblique (that is, in an uncertain world we often end up achieving goals through indirect approaches, not direct ones).

ACTIVITIES FOR REFLECTIVE PRACTICE

1. If you have access to the senior management team in your organisation or business unit, interview them about their opinion of your organisation's source(s) of competitive advantage.

2. What is your own view on this? Be prepared to answer questions they might have for you.

Portfolios and scenario planning

A **MABA** analysis is a high-level tool for determining decisions. It compares the external market attractiveness (MA) – such as profit margins, market size and expected growth, and competitiveness of an offering – with the business attractiveness (BA) – an internal analysis on how much sense the market opportunity makes given present products, services, activities and competencies. The well-known format was developed by McKinsey with GE for use in large organisations with a large number of product or service portfolios.

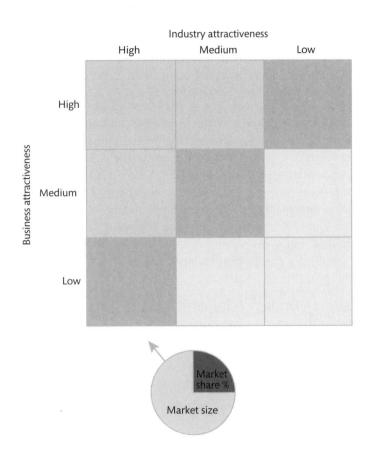

FIGURE 7.1 McKinsey–GE grid
Source: McKinsey & Company in collaboration with General Electric.
Reproduced with permission.

The matrix brings together supply chain and value chains, generic strategies, industry attractiveness models and managerial accounting. To simplify things (sort of), the GE matrix gives each factor a weighting that reflects how it influences either market or business attractiveness. Units in the portfolio are represented by a circle showing the size of the market (size of the circle), share of the market (as a pie chart) and direction of potential in attractiveness (an arrow), as in Figure 7.1.

A MABA analysis is much more than a grid and may involve many steps to complete. It will need to include a lot of educated guesses about segment size and market share potential to be done thoroughly. In fact, for some the main problem is that the choice and weighing of market or business indicators (e.g. margins relative to competitors) is often a matter of opinion. Figures that are based on opinion might look robust but are only as good as the assumptions and the thinking underlying them.

Strategy's uneasy relationship with the future

No plan survives the first encounter with an event it did not foresee. The unpredictability of the future is the Achilles heel of strategic planning. This may be one reason why financial markets respond positively to signals of stability and why many senior managers are cautious when protecting the interests of shareholders. Unpredictability means any plans you make will be risky and companies identify and minimise risk in many ways (we will look at this in the next chapter), so strategic thinking is a balance between visionary thinking and discounting uncertainty.

Following the energy crises of the 1970s, many organisations started to adopt a way of thinking developed by Shell. Scenario planning accepts that the present is no indicator of the future and that uncertainty about what will happen needs to be part of the process. Future events are seen either as predetermined (i.e. already set in motion) or undetermined (i.e. the consequences of events already set in motion). Scenario planning requires the manager to let go of the logic of current thinking and therefore has a lot to do with awareness and critical thinking about how things work. There are three steps:

1. Identify predetermined elements. What is already happening? What are the current trends that will impact the organisation? How are things connected currently?

2. Ask what sorts of uncertainties these relationships could produce.

3. Develop (up to four) alternative scenarios that reflect the effects of variations in specific, identified uncertainties or boundaries.

> scenario planning requires the manager to let go of the logic of current thinking

Scenario planning is a way to structure thinking. Correctly done (which means 'slowly done'), its strength is that it takes into account the open nature of the environment. It requires a clear vision and attention to detail in planning, but encourages you to scan your surroundings.

ACTIVITIES FOR REFLECTIVE PRACTICE

1. What are some of the strengths and limitations of the methods and models for strategy reviewed in this chapter? How have they helped you understand your organisation?

▶

> **2** Reflect on your understanding of strategy. In your organisation, how can you become more involved in strategy:
>
>   (a) Analysis?
>
>   (b) Creation?
>
>   (c) Implementation?

Putting it together: the future is unwritten

Strategy is the search for cohesion, so it is interesting to note how much disagreement there is about its meaning. Perhaps this should not be a surprise. After all, strategy is the subject most associated with sense making and that is not a clear-cut process. In strategy it is often said that the devil is not in the detail, it's in the implementation. So how can you transcend the many debates and escape the myriad traps? Here are a few additional questions to prompt your thinking:

1 Is strategy fully defined? The models and theories in this chapter have been based mostly on activities in large corporations, many based in North America. Do these ideas apply to other parts of the world, or equally well to small and medium-sized companies? What about the public or not-for-profit sectors?

2 Is strategy not the 'grand design' but rather the process of managing tiny feedback loops (known as the iterative process)? Many managers are unhappy with the idea that strategy formulation is a remote process and that planning must precede implementation. Strategy may actually happen at the coal-face.

3 What is the moral dimension of strategy? The standard mantras of competitive advantage and shareholder value have, some would argue, made strategy blind to moral and ethical issues and obsessive about winning.

It is important to raise these questions. International business (the subject of Chapter 9) is influenced by our cultural biases and these in turn influence our theories of business and economics. The link between strategy and values has often been overlooked – it requires a long-term view, not a short-term one. In the end, you need to make up your own mind whether strategy is made on the go or brought about by planning. Only you can decide whether it is limited to meeting corporate goals or has a duty to meet social ones as well. We will look at this again in Part 4, under leadership (Chapter 10) and reputation (Chapter 11).

Further reading

The choice of books on strategy is enormous and it is worth spending some time browsing, so this list is by no means exhaustive:

A classic text:	*The Rise and Fall of Strategic Planning* by Henry Mintzberg (1994), Free Press. The book that challenged many myths in corporate planning.
Going deeper:	*Competitive Strategy: Techniques for analyzing industries and competitors* by Michael E. Porter (2004), Free Press. A clear and concise presentation of Porter's ideas.
Listen to this:	'The Bottom Line' is a business conversation show on BBC Radio 4. It is hosted by Evan Davis and more than 140 past episodes are available at: **www.bbc.co.uk/programmes/b006sz6t/episodes/player**

Notes

1 Drucker, P. (1979) *Management*, Pan Books, p. 445.
2 www.pg.com/en_US/company/purpose_people/pvp.shtml, The Procter &
Gamble Company. Extract reproduced with permission.
3 Porter, M.E. (2004) *Competitive Strategy: Techniques for analyzing
industries and competitors*, New Edition, Free Press.
4 Mintzberg, H. (1978) 'Patterns in strategy formation', *Management Science*,
24(9): 934–948.
5 Porter, M.E. (1979) 'How competitive forces shape strategy', *Harvard
Business Review*, March–April, 57(2): 137–145.
6 Hamel, G. and Prahalad, C.K. (1996) *Competing for the Future*, Harvard
Business School Press.
7 Kay, J. (1993) *Foundations of Corporate Success*, Oxford University Press.

QUESTIONS FOR REFLECTION

1 Do you have any self-limiting beliefs? Try to identify two or three (ask others to tell you if you can't think of any). Write down the assumptions you have made for each belief.

2 Sit still in silence for several minutes. What do you notice going on around you? Write some notes. Make short spells of stillness a new part of your daily practice.

Finance 2: corporate finance and governance

We really can't forecast all that well and yet we pretend that we can but we really can't.

Alan Greenspan, quoted on *The Daily Show*, 2013[1]

In a nutshell

Corporate finance is part of strategic thinking because collectively managers must assess, implement and evaluate a given course of future action in terms of its ability to create or destroy value. The most common metrics used to measure this are financial. In Part 2 we looked at finance in terms of reporting past performance, but this is not the same thing as valuing the business. A business is worth what it can be expected to do in the future. Corporate finance is about systematically choosing a course of action that will create value in the future.

In this chapter you will:

▌ understand how businesses measure value in the future

▌ look at risk and how it may be managed

▌ see how governance structures are set up and work

▌ understand the principles behind and importance of valuation in financial planning

Ensuring the future of the organisation

You don't have to be the manager making the big, strategic decisions for corporate finance to be important. The fact is that you are already involved, because those decisions need implementing and you must align what you do to an overall direction. Look back now at the McKinsey 7-S framework. Imagine how each of those elements needs to be aligned for the organisation to maintain balance. In a similar way, knowing more about why your organisation has the capital structure and investments it does makes it easier for you to understand the purpose of your job. Later in your career it could be you deciding which plans to implement, so an understanding of the language and theory of corporate finance will be crucial then.

> ### ACTIVITIES FOR REFLECTIVE PRACTICE
>
> Arrange to speak with your chief financial officer. Ask them to explain the capital structure of your organisation. What is the balance between equity and debt (gearing)? How is it appropriate to the goals of your organisation?

First we need to restate as plainly as possible what value looks like in finance terms. An organisation with no cash (or access to cash) has no future. It follows that an organisation must be concerned with how it will continue to generate enough cash in the future to fulfil the task of value creation. To do this, senior management has to make three kinds of decision:

1. **Investment**: deciding which projects or assets will produce free cash flows (i.e. investable or distributable returns after adjustment for earnings before taxation) in years to come.

2. **Financial**: deciding where is the best place to source the funding for investment. Is it better to seek new investment from equity or debt, for example?

3 **Dividend**: deciding whether and how cash surpluses
(after other obligations have been paid) should be
redistributed among shareholders, or reinvested.

Sounds straightforward. As you might expect, though, there
are some caveats:

▮ In many free-market economies, shareholder wealth is the
most important measure of value and generating returns
to shareholders is more important than profit. But not all
companies, countries or cultures place shareholder value
so clearly above the interests of other stakeholders. Interest
is growing in alternative models, such as production
cooperatives, mutual societies, collaborative economies
(consumers swapping goods directly with each other) and
Islamic finance.

▮ Numbers feel real, but the quantification of value creation
masks exactly how much human judgement and intuition
are used in financial planning, which is a lot.

▮ Despite systems of safeguards intended to prevent
unethical behaviour, company managers may fail to avoid
temptation and put their own interests first. Corporate
scandals and greed have been in the news all too often.

Nevertheless, wealth creation remains at the heart of
value measurement as it is taught at business school.
Wherever you work, fiduciary duty affects what you do.
So, let's look at corporate finance decisions through five
lenses: governance, valuation, risk management, value and
financing. I will focus on what these concepts mean for you
as a manager in your day-to-day work rather than what they
might mean to an investor (the literature in that area is vast).

> wherever you work, fiduciary duty
> affects what you do

Governance

We saw in Chapter 1 that representing the interests of the owners or founders is a basic management task. Shareholders are supposed to trust that managers will make decisions without the need for constant monitoring, and managers are supposed not to put their own reward ahead of the interests of the shareholders. This responsibility is called fiduciary duty and is a legal relationship between the principal (owner) and agent (manager).

That relationship, called governance, is what is called for in agency theory. In an ideal world – in theory – managers will act only to maximise the interests of owners or shareholders and not to further their own to the detriment of shareholders. Agency theory states that this needs to be governed to make sure that managers don't put their own wealth first. Governance makes sure that activity carried out by managers is not in conflict with owner interests. It tries to mitigate this risk by incentivising senior managers, often with performance-based inducements such as bonuses or shares, to fulfil their fiduciary duty and create value.

It will help to understand the differences between management and governance:

▊ Responsibilities of management:

– Make day-to-day decisions to execute a strategy.

– To 'do things right'.

– Align their actions with the boundaries set by the governing body.

▊ Responsibilities of governance:

– Oversight of the whole organisation and its structures, functions and traditions.

– To 'do the right things'.

- Make sure that objectives are met in an effective and transparent way.
- Hold accountability to stakeholders and the wider community.

Boards are appointed by shareholders to undertake this setting of direction and upholding of values and to monitor and check the work of management. They are not involved in the day-to-day running of the business.

ACTIVITIES FOR REFLECTIVE PRACTICE

What is the governance structure of your organisation? Find out what you can about the people who are in governance roles in your organisation.

CASE STUDY

Pfizer walks away from controversial Astra offer

In early 2014 US pharmaceutical giant Pfizer was repeatedly rebuffed in a 'friendly' takeover by the board of AstraZeneca. This is how the *Financial Times* summed up the news in its weekly review:

> Pfizer's politically controversial £69.4bn pursuit of AstraZeneca came to an end this week with the US pharmaceutical company finally admitting defeat. It abandoned the month-long takeover battle for its British rival two hours before the Monday deadline for a deal to be struck under UK takeover rules.
>
> It marks a rare failure for a company that has prevailed in a series of huge deals in the past 15 years. But it brought relief to UK politicians and scientists who were concerned over the deal's potential impact on AstraZeneca's nearly 7,000-strong UK workforce.

▶

Attention has now switched to whether Pfizer will launch another approach when the mandatory six-month cooling-off period ends, with investors in AstraZeneca, including its largest, BlackRock, signalling a desire for renewed talks. Although Ian Read, Pfizer's chairman and chief executive, gave no clear sign that was likely, he also failed to rule it out.

Both companies have been criticised by shareholders for letting the deal fail, with AstraZeneca accused of rejecting the £55-a-share proposal too hastily, and Pfizer was questioned for declaring the offer as final – making it impossible to raise the bid.

AstraZeneca will now be under intense pressure to deliver promised growth.

Pfizer had planned to shift its tax residence to the UK in the event of a deal – the most high-profile attempt so far by an American multinational group to shelter its offshore revenues from US taxation.

Source: Wilson, N., 'WEEK IN REVIEW – PHARMACEUTICALS – Pfizer walks away from controversial Astra offer', *The Financial Times*, 31 May 2014. © The Financial Times Limited. All Rights Reserved.

What is interesting in this case is that, amid enormous media interest, successive offers from Pfizer were rejected by the AstraZeneca board. While the popular press focused on the emotive politics of a threat to jobs post-merger and loss of British identity in the sector (despite AstraZeneca's global reach and Swedish co-ownership), financial media coverage looked into the governance aspects of the proposed move. The background was analysed from several angles, including strategic marketing (match of respective brand portfolios, access to R&D for new product pipeline), corporate finance (cash flows drying up due to the 'cliff's edge' of expiring patents) and governance (avoiding tax, dividends payments for shareholders, share price).

What made the difference here? It's unlikely to be a question of politics. As many insiders were reported as saying, 'price trumps politics', and any deal – now or in the future – will hang on the vested interests of the shareholders of both companies. Pfizer's long-term strategy may have been to bring together two large companies in order to de-merge them later on and take advantage of the new drug pipeline acquired from AstraZeneca. The story will no doubt continue to evolve.

Valuation

It is a board's responsibility to create value as a return on money invested by shareholders. Therefore they need to understand not just the performance of the business but also how much it is worth – its valuation. They will be the ones who make decisions about buying or selling parts of the business (or acquiring others), so it's vital for them to know what the return is, or will be, as generated by a particular investment. Governance addresses risk (and therefore financial risk) as well as valuation. Management and governance need to coordinate for a business to work well.

> management and governance need to coordinate for a business to work well

Senior management is expected to act to maximise shareholder value and minimise risks found in long-term financial planning. Shareholder value is measured using discounted cash flows (DCF), which allows the organisation to address two questions:

1 Will a given future strategy create value for owners/ shareholders?

2 Which future strategy is better than continuing the
current one?

Because of inflation the value of money will decrease
over time unless invested. Fiduciary duty means that
management must look for, and then be able to justify and
evaluate, the best future plan to create wealth. You may have
many possible courses of action available to you, so you
need a way to compare like with like. The most common
way to do this is by an NPV calculation, which is the total
present worth of a series of future cash flows that has been
discounted at a specified rate.

In finance terms, value is created when companies invest
at returns that exceed the opportunity cost of capital (OCC)
and this is the minimum expectation for any project in
its terminal value at the end of the planning period. OCC
is a key concept in corporate finance because the money
working in one place is missing the 'opportunity' of
working somewhere else and it establishes the measure of
performance of an investment in a commercial organisation.
The time during which economic return exceeds the hurdle
rate (for example, the OCC) is known as the competitive
advantage period (CAP). Beyond CAP, the advantage
diminishes as returns are eroded to a point where no
additional value is being produced. Context means that
what is 'long-term' in one industry may be 'short-term' in
another, and different parts of different businesses assess
things in different ways. Critically, in all cases the past is no
guarantee of the future. A planning period will end with a
hypothetical point at which you expect your competition to
catch up, so to continue to generate value there must then be
further investment, and the cycle goes on.

While these principles are known to all players, there
is enormous scope for qualitative judgement (and
misjudgement) and no amount of number crunching will

replace business acumen and experience. Here is where corporate finance meets the many internal and external forms of analysis featured in earlier chapters.

Calculating a discount rate

The valuation of debt covers borrowings, although here, as with equity, there is complexity and volatility (think about the jungle of traded derivative instruments or the background to the US subprime mortgage collapse in 2007), but since prices for most sources of debt are determined by open-market supply and demand, a market rate is available to determine OCC. The initial basis for that rate is the interest earned on government bonds because they deliver a (virtually) risk-free return.

Any uncertainty about the future represents risk, so adjustments for this will also be built into the calculation of a discount rate. There are three broad categories of metrics:

▌ **Free cash flow**: 'free' because it can be distributed to shareholders, cash is discounted over a known period at the appropriate cost of capital. The time in which any returns are in excess of this capital cost is known as the competitive advantage period.

▌ **Economic profit**: measured by, for example, EVA (Chapter 5) or market value added (MVA).

▌**Cash flow ROI**: a modified internal rate of return (IRR) calculation using cash flows to assess whether investments exceed or fall below the cost of capital.

Risk management

Higher risk suggests higher return, which in most for-profit companies is an attractive proposition. It also has a downside, of course, if the venture fails to produce returns. The future value of risk is therefore reflected in calculations of the cost of capital. Financial economists distinguish between two types of risk:

1 **Unsystemic**, which is inherently present in a particular industry, sector, company or even in a narrow set of stocks.

2 **Systemic** (aggregate), which is the instability inherent in the market as a whole. Volatility is a systemic risk: the amount by which returns on an asset may vary over time. The more it varies and the more difficult this variation is to predict, the lower the value of the asset in the present time. The measurement of an asset's systemic volatility is a comparison of asset return to market return and this is known as the beta (i.e. how much it moved, or didn't move, with the market in the past). Interest rates, economic cycles and day-trading are all sources of systemic risk on stock markets.

As nervous entrepreneurs pitching unrealistic valuations on the popular TV show *Dragons' Den* often find to their cost, the value of a company is tied to future cash flows. Every business is different, but management must take into account all the risk factors appropriate to its sector, size and life-cycle maturity, as well as the whole host of internal and external concerns that we looked at in earlier chapters.

Investment decisions: SVA

Shareholder value analysis (SVA) is what corporate finance has substituted for traditional business measurements in many parts of the world. Shareholders' capital is supposed to earn a higher return than by investing in other assets with the same amount of risk. If a company sees equity returns higher than equity costs, value is created. When that value is known, the organisation can act on this to improve its performance, as well as work out how successful past projects have been. Shareholder value can be determined by discounting the expected cash flows to the present at the weighted average cost of capital. So far we have looked at finance only from the perspective of for-profit enterprises, which aim at generating free cash flows for their owners or shareholders.

The investment side of corporate finance covers stocks, shares and financial markets for managing investments and risk and would take more than a section in this book to cover. Since our focus is on the types of decisions middle and senior management need to make internally, knowing how a particular investment or project is attractive in value terms is more important.

The attractiveness of a proposed course of future strategic action is determined by its discounted cash flows. This brings us back to the capital structure of an organisation and to the weighted average cost of capital (WACC), which is a calculation of opportunity costs averaged across the capital structure of the organisation, reflecting the risks associated with debt and equity. WACC is a calculation of the percentage and cost of debt plus the percentage and cost of equity. The function of a corporate WACC is as a discount rate. In other words, the level of return on capital needed for an investment must be better than employing that debt or equity elsewhere. This approach is part of value-based management (VBM).

VBM, though, is under severe scrutiny following the near collapse of the economic system in many of the world's mature economies. When all that matters is that every decision is evaluated in terms of the effect on shareholder wealth, the dynamic between the owners and the managers acting on their behalf is thrown into sharp contrast.

It is worth noting here that things are a little different in the case of not-for-profits (e.g. community groups, charitable trusts, non-governmental organisations (NGOs), social enterprises), where the aim is not to accrue wealth but to serve the aims of members by maximising the marginal effect of operations on the capital donated. Value here means human well-being. Can this still be measured by cash flows? Not exactly, but the idea of the time value of money is still useful to evaluate competing options for long- or short-term welfare benefits.

> value here means human well-being. Can this still be measured by cash flows?

In many countries, the funding of the health care sector (especially if it is a public service funded by the state) is a significant – and complex – subset of valuation because it is not always obvious how to put a monetary value on health benefits. Should only the costs of interventions be compared, or rather costs versus benefits?

SMEs cannot generate the kind of data for the capital assets pricing model (CAPM) or for beta calculations, so the quickest solution is to replace many of the variable elements of SVA with market-driven substitutes (for example, by identifying and using the betas of traded companies with similar debt/equity ratios and similar economic influences). Value in SMEs is a broader concept than in traded companies, so the market value is often seen as being the price the owners would get if they were to sell the company. That may be arrived at by:

1. valuing the firm's assets, which usually indicates the business is not viable and needs to be broken up

2. comparing what similar companies are worth (rather like valuing your house by looking at house prices around you)

3. expected future income. This last one is the most common, but may take into account all sorts of other factors, such as competitive position, industry life cycle, type of customer base, scalability of the business and so on.

ACTIVITIES FOR REFLECTIVE PRACTICE

1. How good do you think the discounted cash flow method is for valuing a not-for-profit?

2. What role do you think the personality of the owners plays in valuing an SME?

Financial planning

Financial planning combines strategic decision making with the capital structure of the whole organisation into the future. Chapter 5 established where this process begins – with awareness of the current situation using financial statements and ratios. There is a lot of wriggle room for interpretation in statistics and ratios, so when it comes to planning rather than formulaic answers, you want this information to provide good, common-sense questions about the long term. When you get down to it, planning for the long term (i.e. beyond the coming 12 months) involves the following:

▌ **Preparing for contingencies**: 'what ifs' are the difference between simple forecasting and scenario planning (Chapter 7).

▌ **Weighing up all the angles**: a strategic direction may not always be set with only one thing in mind. A move in a new direction may have non-financial imperatives, such as laying the groundwork now in something that enables other, future steps.

▌ **Bringing it all together**: properly done and clearly communicated, long-term plans can unify by providing a perspective for all parts of an organisation and by linking the consequences of managerial decisions at all levels.

We've seen that the main sources of funding for future growth and investment are equity and debt.

Equity is money invested in the business by shareholders, usually in the form of shares. Additional money may be raised by the sale of new shares and usually this is in the expectation that funds will go towards non-current assets. Equity attracts returns in the future through payments of dividends from excess residual funds, but equity holders carry more risk (they are not first in line for repayment) so will expect a higher rate of return, which they will also discount to present value to make sure it is invested well. Shareholders are closer to the running of a business than financial institutions, so this can bring additional pressure to bear on senior management to aim for short-term gains.

Debt, meanwhile, is money lent to the business by investors or financial institutions without the expectation of a say in the aims or purpose of the business. Debt offers a fixed claim to interest payments and may offer a slightly lower cost of capital than equity because the lender knows that they have preferred status for repayment. Finding the right balance of long-term funding is not easy. Many companies try to match long-term assets to long-term borrowings or equity, but prefer to maintain liquidity in working capital financed from inventories or short-term securities.

> **finding the right balance of long-term funding is not easy**

Capital budgeting is the annual listing of major investment projects and these are expenditures that will, presumably, bring some future benefit if properly implemented. All such decisions must consider:

- the current and future composition of the organisation's capital structure
- whether the size and balance of current asset structure is right for the expected returns, and how that structure should change in the future
- the size of funding needed to finance future asset structure.

The ratios mentioned in Chapter 5 can be useful in addressing some of these issues because they are all in relationship with the capital structure. What you as a general manager are looking for is:

1 a way of explaining present and past performance, and

2 assessment of risk and return in future activity.

This leads to the further question of the best sources of capital, because as we have seen above, equity and debt carry different costs and can have implications for valuation. All of these options will produce changes to the capital structure, which is why it is important to find out from your finance staff what is appropriate for your organisation.

Organisations may change their capital structure in more radical ways. Here are just a few:

▌ **Merger or acquisition**: Legally, a merger is the creation of a third entity from the coming together of two others and an acquisition is the new ownership of one organisation by another. However, the distinction is often blurred, as what occurs in law can be very different to what is experienced by all those concerned.

▌ **Leveraged buyout (LBO)**: A (private) takeover funded mostly with debt from institutional investors, usually as a prelude to the rapid sale or radical reorganisation of assets. Collateral comes from the expected cash flows or existing assets of the target.

▌ **Spin-off**: This is when a potentially profitable part of a going concern is sold off as a separate business with, initially, identical ownership structure (and perhaps management team as well) in both old and new.

▌ **Carve-off/divestment**: A privatisation would be an example of this in the public sector, but in the private sector it can usually indicate the removal by sale of unwanted assets. Reasons for doing this may vary, but often include a wish to return to a particular core competence or activity, indication of under-performance of a part of a portfolio, fundraising, or as a requirement imposed by regulatory bodies.

▌ **Bankruptcy**: A legal status that indicates the inability (of a person) to pay one's creditors. However, when applied to the 'corporate person' bankruptcy may indicate a more subtle and controlled (protected) relationship with creditors whereby commercial activity may continue. This form of arrangement may vary from one country to another.

Putting it together: governance in an age of market failure

Corporate governance is what ties together the various
strands in this chapter. Governance and agency theory refer
to the structures in place in an organisation to represent
and protect the interests of owners and shareholders. If the
agent possesses asymmetrical information of a kind that
may damage or destroy shareholder value, it could lead to
dilemmas, such as:

▌ **moral hazard**: behaviour that takes advantage of
asymmetric information after a transaction

▌ **conflict of interest**: behaviour of an individual due to
multiple interests, at least one of which is in direct
opposition to the interests of the principal (owner).

In some countries governance of larger, publicly traded
companies is legislated for and codified. Structures that
organisations put in place to mitigate the risks of governance
failures include managerial incentive schemes, takeovers,
board of directors, pressure from institutional investor,
product market competition and organisational structure,
all of which can be thought of as constraints that affect the
process through which risk and returns are distributed.

Further reading

A classic text: *The Wealth of Nations* by Adam
Smith (1982), Penguin Classics. The
book that brought us 'the invisible
hand' and 'the division of labour',
Smith's 200-year-old classic was one
of the first explorations of the market
economy.

Going deeper: *23 Things They Don't Tell You
About Capitalism* by Ha-Joon Chang
(2011), Penguin Books. An accessible,
thought-provoking and well-researched
presentation of a macroeconomic
viewpoint that challenges many of our
norms.

Watch this: 'Sir Adrian Cadbury reflects on
properly constituted audit committees
and boardroom self-evaluation.'
An interview with the chair of the
Cadbury Committee on corporate
governance, part of the wide range of
additional business materials freely
available online: **http://youtu.be/
ZfC7ykLKy4M**

Note

1 www.businessinsider.com/alan-greenspan-on-the-daily-show-2013-10

QUESTIONS FOR REFLECTION

1 Reflect on the best and worst pieces of financial advice
that you have received in your life, or your best and
worst experiences with money. What advice would you
pass on to others?

2 Do you have a long-term financial plan? Do you want to
retire in the traditional sense? What do you see yourself
doing at that age?

Global and international business

> *The major uncertainty facing the world today is not the Euro but the future direction of China. The growth model for its rapid rise has run out of steam.*
>
> George Soros (writing at the end of 2013)[1]

In a nutshell

When your daily work is dominated by tactical thinking, globalisation and international business can seem like remote concerns. Don't be deceived though. You are already part of the global economy, even if you work in a small organisation with no apparent multinational involvement.

This chapter looks at two things. First, macroeconomics and the terms used in policy making for nations, groups of nations and institutions that regulate international trade. Then, a survey of multinational enterprises (MNEs), which are corporations with headquarters in one country and networks of subsidiary, affiliate or acquired companies that are hosted in others.

In this chapter you will:

▌ define key macroeconomic terms and theories

▌ look at the nature of the international business environment

▌ understand how the global market forces and firms shape strategic thinking

▌ see how organisations measure international competitive advantage and choose channels for growth

How beautiful is big?

Take a look at Table 9.1 showing Fortune's top 20 global companies ranked by 2013 turnover. Do you recognise all the names? If not, you may want to look them up. Once you have found out who they all are, what strikes you about the list?

You may have noticed the number of energy companies represented (7 of the top 10). Not long ago, this top 20 would have been a balance of oil and gas producers, manufacturers and financial institutions. That's one aspect, and here is another: the 2005 Fortune 500 Global list contained a total of 16 Chinese companies; in 2013 it contained 89. The balance of the world economy is shifting – new markets are not just opening up, they represent whole new ways of doing business.

In number and in magnitude, MNEs have ballooned in the last 60 years, thanks to regional waves of privatisation, economic liberalisation and market deregulation. In fact, MNEs now account for the majority of the economic activity in the world and embody in practice much of what is taught on an MBA. They embody power, too, driving foreign direct investment and supporting first and second tiers of supplier companies. Multinationals have clout, so when international

TABLE 9.1 Fortune's top 20 global companies ranked by 2013 turnover

Rank	Name	Revenues ($ bn)	Profit ($ bn)
1	Royal Dutch Shell	481.7	26.6
2	Wal-Mart Stores	469.2	17.0
3	Exxon Mobil	449.9	44.9
4	Sinopec Group	428.2	8.2
5	China National Petroleum	408.6	18.2
6	BP	388.3	11.6
7	State Grid	298.4	12.3
8	Toyota Motor	265.7	11.6
9	Volkswagen	247.6	27.9
10	Total	234.3	13.7
11	Chevron	233.9	26.2
12	Glencore Xstrata	214.4	1.0
13	Japan Post Holdings	190.9	6.8
14	Samsung Electronics	178.6	20.6
15	E.ON	169.8	2.8
16	Phillips 66	169.6	4.1
17	ENI	167.9	10.0
18	Berkshire Hathaway	162.5	14.8
19	Apple	156.5	41.7
20	AXA	154.6	5.3

Source: Fortune Global 500, 2013

companies fail, the fallout can be spectacular. Here are three examples:

▌ When Enron imploded in 2001, it was standing on a pedestal in the top 10 of US companies. Many investors, staff and customers were left with nothing.

▌ By 2014 the cost to BP of the 2010 disaster on the Deepwater Horizon platform, on which 11 lives were lost and from which 5 million barrels of oil spilled into the Gulf of Mexico, had passed the $42 billion mark. The company, the sixth largest in the world, has faced severe criticism of its response, governance structure and leadership.

▌ The credit crunch of 2008–9 that was precipitated by the US subprime mortgage collapse in 2007 threatened many of the word's global banking institutions. US bank Lehman Brothers filed for bankruptcy in 2008, triggering a banking crisis and prompting national and regional governments around the world to begin a lengthy and painful series of measures to intervene and bail out a series of private, global banks.

Corporate failure happens all the time, of course. Most new ventures fail, and many businesses go through a life cycle that results in maturity and decline (or acquisition). Despite the enormous number of companies in the world, we mostly examine either the big (too big to fail?) survivor stories (and base our management theories on them, too) or the spectacular failure stories. Little attention is paid to what lies in the middle.

Even less attention is paid to the dynamics of the ecology of the whole population of organisations. Corporate failure, even among multinational giants, can have positive repercussions. When Nokia, at one time the world's largest supplier of mobile phone handsets, was surpassed by its competitors and went into decline, the company cut its global workforce by 24,000 and sold its mobile phone business to Microsoft in a deal worth more than $7 billion. The aftermath of this turmoil and headcount reduction in Nokia's home country of Finland has been a resurgence of high-tech company start-ups.

> corporate failure, even among multinational giants, can have positive repercussions

ACTIVITIES FOR REFLECTIVE PRACTICE

All companies need to experience growth when they start and we have become used to the idea that one purpose of a business is to get bigger.

1. For you, is growth a question of maxima (constantly getting larger) or optima (reaching an ideal size)?

2. Does your organisation have an ideal size, or should it keep growing?

The question posed for managers by globalisation is to understand the role and purpose of business as it relates to the macroeconomic environment. Later in this chapter I want to consider how firms act in the international business environment, but first let's take a look at some macro-level economic principles.

Macroeconomics

Macroeconomics is the study of the economy as a whole. It is the basis for long-term policies and interventions that promote development (growth) and limit the impact of economic cycles. Like all aspects of economics it is concerned with scarcity of resources, but on a much wider scale than the micro world of the organisation.

Several hundred years ago, wealth creation meant the wealth of nations rather than shareholders. The nation-state preceded the corporation as the unit of analysis. The idea was first developed by Adam Smith in 1776, and still has an attraction for some economists who study at the comparative advantage of one country over another in the production and trade of various types of goods or commodities. The metric (and rule of thumb) most often used for the economic activity of a country is its gross domestic product (GDP), the total output of goods and services for a given territory and time. Simplified, GDP looks at household spending, investment and consumer confidence, government spending, and volumes of exports/imports. Regional aggregates of GDP are telling. In 2012 the combined GDP of the G7[2] economies was $33,932 billion (47 per cent of the world total). By comparison, the same figure for the whole of sub-Saharan Africa (49 countries) was $1,273 billion (1.8 per cent of total).[3]

Macroeconomists are as interested in supply and demand, pricing and the supply of money as are microeconomists, but at an aggregated level. Money supply and demand/supply of goods are the basic ingredients for inflation and are all connected in complex flows of rise and fall in outputs, prices and international trade.

National competitiveness and economic growth

The modern corporation did not begin to emerge until the end of the nineteenth century. Historically, large and powerful trading corporations, such as the British East India Company, grew from the patronage of state, monarchy and colonial military ambition. In the 17th and 18th centuries, amid powerful advancements in science, production and economics in Europe following the Enlightenment, East India trading companies were set up to exploit Austrian, Dutch, Danish, French, Portuguese and Swedish national ambitions of trade with Asia.

The World Trade Organization (WTO) was set up in 1995 and coordinates trade agreements and negotiations among 159 member countries. It has promoted the removal of many barriers to trade and (controlled) freedom of movement of capital and labour has superseded the protectionist outlook that dominated before the 1970s. In fact, few countries can now afford to act in their own interests without being part of international (regional) trade agreements such as NAFTA (North American Free Trade Association), the EU (European Union) or ASEAN (Association of Southeast Asian Nations). Economically everyone is connected. In 2001 former Goldman Sachs chairman Jim O'Neill coined the acronym BRIC to highlight the importance of four emerging economies (Brazil, Russia, India and China) to the global economy in the coming 50 years. Recently he has come up with MINT, four countries (Mexico, Indonesia, Nigeria and Turkey) identified as the next centres of economic growth. Transnational organisations such as the IMF or the World Bank act as checks and balances on the flow and supply of money:

▌ **Fiscal policy (demand side)**: the tactical or strategic use by governments of revenues and taxes in public expenditure to influence key macroeconomic factors such as employment, investment and industrial output.

▌ **Monetary policy (supply side)**: the use (most typically) by central banks of interest rates to influence inflation, with the aim of maintaining economic stability in the medium and long term.

▌ **Trade and exchange rate policy**: increasingly being coordinated by members of the trading blocs, though severely under scrutiny following the subprime mortgage collapse in the US, the euro crisis in the EU and a decade of stagnation in Japan.

It's worth restating that most of the world's economies are based on capitalism, albeit in several forms. China, with a communist political system, has been fairly clear about the role of market capital in the economy since the 1990s.

The international business environment

Senior management needs to look at the macro factors in their environment that can influence their primary goals, or that might advantage their competitors. In the previous chapter we looked at this through the lens of a PESTEL. This is usually applied from the point of view of a single organisation as it looks outwards, but for the student of international business, a PESTEL is applied to the whole industry or sector, as in the example in Figure 9.1 for the airline industry.

> ▌ senior management needs to look at the macro factors in their environment

A PESTEL must recognise the importance of the political and technological factors in the past, but really hints at the importance of social shifts and macroeconomic trends that will bring volatility for the future. For example, margins in the airline industry have been wafer-thin for some years, so identifying the right market to ensure a higher marginal return may be the primary task.

Political	Deregulation of air travel in Europe and US, decline of support for 'national flag' airlines, legacy of 9/11
Economic	Globalisation, economic cycles of boom and bust, credit crunch of 2008, emerging markets in Asia, fuel costs
Social	Passenger demographics, growing middle class in Asia, tourism, business travel, threats from terrorism
Technological	Growth of online commerce, economies of scale from mergers and acquisitions, new plane sizes, reliability, efficiency
Environmental	Effects of aviation on pollution levels, carbon off-setting, effects of tourism in certain locations
Legal	Variety of legislation affecting noise, aviation tax and passenger legal rights (e.g. the EU)

FIGURE 9.1 PESTEL analysis of the international airline industry

ACTIVITIES FOR REFLECTIVE PRACTICE

1 Construct a PESTEL analysis of the widest possible environment as it affects your industry.

2 Which elements stand out to you as being more important? What should all organisations in your industry be paying most attention to?

There are three sets of questions to ask about international business:

1 Why do businesses move outside their original national borders? What is the motivation?

2 How do they enable themselves to do this? What channels are available?

3 Which is the right channel to become international? Why do different firms choose different ways?

It is estimated that the world's largest 500 MNEs now account for about 80 per cent of the world's foreign direct investment (FDI) and that 75 per cent of these companies are headquartered somewhere in the 'triad' of the US, the EU or Japan.[4] Why might this be so? Michael Porter looks to answer this question using an extension of his thinking on industry competitive advantage. The Porter diamond in Figure 9.2 is the result of research into what appeared to be the reasons for success among companies in clusters of industry types and locations.

The six aspects form an overall framework for analysis. Four are potential determinants of advantage and they interact and influence each other, while the two external variables of government and chance act on these determinants:

▌ **Factor conditions**: include those human, physical and capital resources available as supply of inputs in a location.

▌ **Demand conditions**: include market size, segmentation and access to consumers.

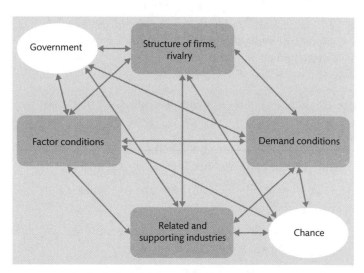

FIGURE 9.2 Porter's diamond model of competitive advantage
Source: Porter, M.E. (1990) *The Competitive Advantage of Nations*, Free Press. With the permission of The Free Press, a Division of Simon & Schuster, Inc., all rights reserved.

▌ **Related/supporting industries**: mainly seen in terms of partners in the supply chain of inputs.

▌ **Structure of firms and rivalry**: Porter believed that the presence of intense rivalry was the most important aspect driving the others.

The main criticism of Porter's diamond is that it analyses a situation using only the conditions in the host country. American academic Alan Rugman doubled the diamond in order to include determinants from both the home and host country. He suggested that the firm should consider both as one if you want a strong basis for building a regional or even a global business.[5]

Globalisation is sometimes confused with international business, but it is a bit more than that. It is the concept of a completely integrated, homogeneous and open worldwide economic system in which inequalities are gradually removed by economic development. Not only is that going to be very hard to measure, even as an ideal it is far from current reality because it is evident that large parts of the world, and most notably Africa, are comparatively poor. Globalisation is a study (by optimists or by pessimists) of barriers, tariffs and segmentation, and of the exploitation of economic or political inequalities for economic gain, and is therefore an aspect we will consider in Chapter 11.

> ▌ globalisation is sometimes confused with international business, but it is a bit more than that

For now, on closer inspection the majority of the world's MNEs may be said to have regional strategies, not truly global ones.

Toyota withdraws production from Australia

After 50 years of production in Australia, in February 2014 Japan's leading car manufacturer, Toyota, made public its decision to end vehicle and engine manufacturing there by 2017. The news followed similar decisions by Mitsubishi, Ford and Holden (General Motors) and came as a severe blow to Australia's business and political confidence and reputation. The exit marked the end of all automotive production in the country.

Akio Toyoda, Toyota's president, was reported in the *Financial Times* in February 2014 as saying that 'various negative factors such as an extremely competitive market and a strong Australian dollar ... have forced us to make this painful decision'.

Toyota's decision is part of a context of a worsening economic climate in Australia, which had avoided the worst effects of the global credit crisis in the years following 2008, seeing successive waves of government investment to prop up an increasingly fragile manufacturing sector. The country's reliance on its mineral wealth and exports to, especially, China had only exaggerated the underlying imbalance.

Toyota claims it had done everything possible to avoid having to close its operations but in the end a combination of macro- and microeconomic factors proved too much to keep production of around 100,000 cars each year viable, 75 per cent of which was for export. Perhaps more significant for the sector is that despite a long decline, many more people work in tier one or tier two automotive suppliers, and many of those jobs and companies will face problems as a result.

The macroeconomic factors influencing Toyota's decision
may have included:

1 Appreciation of the Australian dollar against the US dollar
between 2009 and 2012, making imports more attractive.

2 Increases in wage costs of more than 60 per cent in the
last decade, and much higher than in other developed
economies.

3 A boom in investment in the mining sector.

4 Political pressure for further government subsidies aimed
specifically at propping up the manufacturing sector and
protecting jobs.

Source: Smyth, J. and Wembridge, M. 'Toyota caps off carmaker
exodus from Australia', *The Financial Times*, 10 February 2014.

Toyota's decision is indicative of the ebb and flow of
international trade and investment. Returning to the main
question of why and how domestic organisations become
international ones in the first place, two perspectives
provide some answers.

The macroeconomic approach

FDI was once seen as the rational search by a company for
a superior return on its capital employed by making an
investment overseas. In practice, it's often a lot more than
capital that is invested, and in a lot more than just equity.
Investment involves expanding a portfolio of business
interests, blurring the boundaries between domestic and
international:

■ Supply-side reasons may explain MNEs moving location to
where it costs less to produce.

■ Equally, a demand-side wish to exploit untapped markets
may be the reason.

▌An MNE can take advantage of lower material costs in one place while out-supplying local competitors in their own market somewhere else.

▌The removal of, or special exemption from, tariffs and trade barriers may be a key driver as large firms then move in.

▌MNEs are often able to access much cheaper financing than local firms and their capital structure allows low-cost debt in strong currencies to trade in markets with weak ones. Because capital markets and national economies are cyclical and volatile, this may explain short-term cycles of takeovers.

Macroeconomic theory suggests that MNEs can also be explained by comparative advantage, that is, countries exporting and importing to capitalise on relative strengths and weaknesses in their available national resources or markets. For this reason, MNEs go where there is an efficient supply (for that country) of resource or labour.

The microeconomic approach

This tries to explain the MNE more in terms of the thinking that goes on inside the organisation. Senior management teams:

▌are duty-bound to re-invest for growth wherever there is a better net return to be found, or they will physically follow where their market is growing. What starts out as a success in one market then moves to export to another, which in turn leads to competition and the need to adopt a suitable strategy for internationalisation

▌are culturally better informed by their experience of foreign markets in general and this encourages MNEs to spread

are trained to look for opportunities where a monopolistic or oligopolistic competitive advantage can be gained. This follows the idea that perfect competition cannot really ever exist – there will (even only for historical reasons) always be differentiation and inequalities in markets. The organisation that is best attuned to these is the one best placed to grow and expand, taking advantage of the economies of scale being an MNE can provide.

Economies of scale become standardisation, which in turn allows localisation of a central idea with adaptation (at a lower cost than a local provider can match) of goods and services in new markets. In short, managers use their knowledge of business administration principles to create value by choosing the lowest-cost location for any activity and grow by direct ownership of these assets (as long as the benefits outweigh the costs). Here we begin to understand the activities of MNEs as just an extension of the efficient management of resources outlined in all the chapters of Part 2.

Managing the two levels

This tension between seeing things from either a national or an organisational perspective is expressed in terms of one framework, the CSA–FSA matrix. CSA stands for country-specific advantages, which are those strengths such as geographic location, government policies, natural resources, human resources or levels of technology that nation-states may be said to possess or have access to. FSA refers to firm-specific advantages, or factors traditionally counted as strengths within a company or organisation (many of which we have been looking at in earlier chapters). Occasionally, the boundaries between the two become confused. The East India Company, Russian natural gas provider Gazprom and (at least until 2009) General Motors might all claim to represent something at both levels of structure and strategy.

John Dunning, a leading authority on the theory of the multinational firm, summed up many of these aspects into three types of advantages that determine why and how firms go international – ownership, location or internalisation (OLI).[6] Ownership advantages are basically the same as the FSA features, while location advantages map closely to CSA. Internalisation advantages reflect how an organisation chooses to act on those perceived sets of advantages. Which routes or channels a firm should use to internationalise was, for Dunning, a question of best net return once all risk factors have been taken into account (as we saw in Chapter 8). Just because you can, it doesn't mean you have to – expansion should not be a matter simply of a rush into new markets with capital investment unless alternatives can be shown to be less effective.

> expansion should not be a matter simply of a rush into new markets with capital investment

ACTIVITIES FOR REFLECTIVE PRACTICE

1. Research organisations similar to yours in other countries. What can you say about the strategies they are using?

2. What is the likelihood of the organisation you work for expanding beyond its current size and borders in the next ten years? What would be the best route to do so?

Putting it together: four routes to internationalisation

There are four main routes that an organisation can use to move its scope beyond the borders of its home country:

▌**Export**. Usually the first channel to try, this form of trade is 'as old as the hills'. Exporting represents the lowest risk but is susceptible to government tariff policies, the power that any intermediaries might exert and exchange rate risk as currencies move in relation to each other.

▌**Licence**: Permission or rights given to a partner in the host country, in return for a fee, to trade in the (intellectual) property of the home company. The licensee often carries the majority of the costs and risk, but may also take a larger proportion of the margin than a distributor for an export.

▌**Contractual agreements/joint venture (JV)**: A JV may be the most sensible step into new markets in territories that are developing or emerging, or towards the sharing of know-how in preparation for closer cooperation. Finding a good match with a JV partner in terms of size, ambition and culture is really important. High levels of patience and trust are required. Many JVs fail because the time horizons set for them are too short to build a relationship.

▌**Foreign direct investment**: Ownership of the entity and its assets in the host country, with consequent transfer and flow of home capital, know-how and (at least to begin with) management personnel. FDI may be via acquisition or green-field investment and gives the highest level of control – at the expense of agility or flexibility in exit. FDI is the most costly strategy, so any such transaction costs associated with the extra need to be less than the net advantage gained.

In reality, firms may employ more than one route or strategy, and the intricacies of international trade and tax regulation mean things are rarely as clear-cut as the theory would suggest.

Further reading

A classic text:	*Managing Across Borders: The transnational solution* by Christopher Bartlett and Sumantra Ghoshal (2nd Edition, 2002), Harvard Business School Press.
Going deeper:	*How Do We Fix This Mess? The economic price of having it all, and the route to lasting prosperity* by Robert Peston (2013), Hodder Paperbacks. Peston is a BBC journalist and regular commentator on economic affairs.
Watch this:	'Actually, the world isn't flat.' The 2012 TED talk by Pankaj Ghemawat that cautions us to be more precise when we conjecture about globalisation: **www.ted.com/talks/ pankaj_ghemawat_actually_the_world_ isn_t_flat**

Notes

1 Soros, G (2013) *The Shifting World Economy, Reversing Gears: year in review 2013*, Project Syndicate.

2 Canada, France, the US, Italy, Japan, the UK and Germany.

3 *The Economist Yearbook*, 2014.

4 http://unctad.org/en/Pages/DIAE/World%20Investment%20Report/World_ Investment_Report.aspx

5 Rugman, A.M. and Collinson, S. (2012) *International Business*, 6th Edition, Pearson.

6 Dunning, J.H. (1977) 'Trade, location of economic activity and the MNE: A search for an eclectic approach', in Ohlin, B. Hesselborn, P and Magnus, P. (eds), *The International Allocation of Economic Activity*, Macmillan.

QUESTIONS FOR REFLECTION

'Worldview' is your fundamental orientation, embedded in collective culture, shared language and individual experience, covering all your basic beliefs.

1 What is your worldview? Are you a global corporate citizen?

2 Think about your current work colleagues. What worldviews and perspectives exist among them? Do you understand those viewpoints? Can you hold your view and their views at the same time?

part

Critical MBA thinking: how to master management

Critical n. [ˈkrɪtɪk(ə)l]: careful, thoughtful and exact examination of the assumptions and structure of an argument

The final part of *The Every Day MBA* is about demonstration of mastery of choice in management practice. Tactical thinking is learned on the job, in trial and error as well as by apprenticeship. It helps managers align the parts of the organisation they are responsible for with the strategic goals set from above. Sometimes, as happened early in the story of Swedish furniture company IKEA, a tactical action (removing the legs of tables to fit them into a delivery truck) leads to a strategy, but usually tactical thinking comes later and remains uncritical of the assumptions behind strategic thinking.

Strategic thinking is endlessly analysed and studied at business school. It is how managers establish a direction and set of plans for the future, and it drives the majority of the theories and models of management. A good MBA will bring you this far. A great one will require you to go one step further.

Problems in management do not come in neat boxes marked 'people', 'marketing' or 'finance', etc. The segmentation of business administration into subjects, silos or departments may be convenient, but it is also arbitrary. There are good and bad ways of making this division and the way to find out which is which is by critical thinking.

But critical thinking is used in different ways. It can mean:

▌ systematically solving a problem: either as a way of developing analytical problem-solving skills through the use of real-world examples or as a method of teaching using the method of 'question and answer' to show the shortcomings of an argument. Being critical in problem solving is important, but doesn't often make a transformative difference to you as a manager (or as a person)

▌ questioning and changing unjust social structures: a concern for democratic principles, social progress and justice, and often the uncovering of power relations and inequalities or imbalances in human relations

▌ seeing the world holistically: a systemic view of the relationship between management and our environment. The purpose of this is to release you from *lineal* thinking in problem solving and to reach maturity in how you manage the dilemmas and uncertainties inherent in all management contexts.

Being critical means surfacing deep-set assumptions that you and others hold. For this, we will look at three things:

1 leadership

2 corporate reputation, social responsibility and sustainability

3 reflective practice.

Each is integral to changing your thinking and developing your self-awareness, the two lasting benefits of doing an MBA mentioned in Chapter 1.

Leadership

For we were born only yesterday and know nothing,
and our days on earth are but a shadow.

Book of Job 8:9

In a nutshell

Of all the subjects in _The Every Day MBA_, leadership
holds the greatest promise for both personal learning and
organisational development. Our culture has given us a
number of iconic ideas and images around leadership, yet
we have found it very difficult to agree on one definition.
Management organises what is already there and uses this
to make plans for what is to come. Leadership, meanwhile,
actively steers towards a future that would not just happen
by management alone. It is a conscious, deliberate movement
from the known to the unexplored and untested. Leadership
is relational. It is just as much about followers as it is about
leaders.

Because of its transformational potential, I want you to
think critically about leadership and this means deliberately
questioning some of the assumptions behind the beliefs that
you and others hold.

In this chapter you will:

▌ understand the different ways of defining leadership

▌ establish a difference between managing and leading

▌ review the main theories and models of leadership

▌ contrast the traditional view of the leader with a systemic view of leadership

Why talk about leadership?

It's a truism that the need for good leadership has never been greater. But no one can deny that our interest in leadership is also at an all-time high. There are three reasons why:

1 **It is relevant.** Our general belief is that we live in increasingly complex and challenging times. In the next 10, 20 or 30 years, sustainability, economic emergence of the developing world, population growth, poverty and environmental concerns, geo-politics and demands on scarce resources – as well as ideological diversity in management itself – will all require a response.

2 **There is a demand.** Organisations in emerging economies will be switching from manufacturing to knowledge. Value is now less anchored to tangible assets. As companies grow by acquisition and merger, they will look for 'figureheads' who can influence other people's behaviours.

3 **There is also a supply.** Organisations need leadership and being placed in the role of leader brings that individual influence and authority, which is a popular idea in our culture. Leadership is flavour of the month and a goal for all aspiring managers. The cult of the leader can have a toxic side, too: leaders can be seen as both the solution and the problem. But perhaps this means we should not look for leadership only in the personality of the leader.

Are you a manager or a leader?

It doesn't take long for this question to come up at business school. But it's one that assumes that we already know what sort of a thing leadership is. People have enjoyed debating this since well before anyone started talking about management as a distinct activity and it is fair to say that no one has yet come up with a definitive answer. This chapter will consider the development of leadership, the key concepts and theories, and how they are applied to change in organisations.

Broadly, there are four major perspectives on leadership:

- **Authority and hierarchy**: This views leadership as granted to those naturally best suited to it. This may be down to certain traits or innate qualities, or simply the product of position in society. Being born into or being naturally suited for leadership is perhaps the oldest view – and it explains why leadership training was once an elite and exclusive type of education.

- **Learned competencies**: This sees leadership as a profession, and people can and need to be prepared (trained up) to lead others whenever called upon to do so. Different personalities may develop different leadership styles, but it is definitely a learnable skill, even a profession.

- **Activities, tasks and practice**: Leadership is whatever needs to be done when there is a collective need to overcome a challenge, problem or crisis. In other words, it is a need that brings the leader, not the other way round. There is often a belief that 'the right person for the task' is important, so a link to competencies is maintained.

- **Systemic**: Complexity may look messy, but from a holistic view studying leaders in isolation is half-baked; a bit like studying a marriage only by observing one person. Without

followers there are no leaders and vice versa; the concept
of leadership makes no sense except in context. Systems
thinking suggests that leadership is defined in wider
systems.

The first three cover the conventional views of leadership
in management today, especially in large organisations, and
they have in common that leadership can be understood
by studying what leaders do, or who leaders are. In other
words, you need to understand the individual. Only the
fourth, the systemic view, does not isolate the leader from
the context of leadership.

> leadership can be understood by
> studying what leaders do, or who
> leaders are

In summary, some theories focus on the skill, tactics and
characteristics of people, while others try to understand
what leadership is by seeing how it emerges from a context
or situation. In both cases, however, the contrast between
managing and leading is the next thing to consider.

ACTIVITIES FOR REFLECTIVE PRACTICE

1 Before you read the next section, consider your
thoughts on the question 'Am I a manager or a leader?'

2 Which of the four schools of thought above on the
nature of leadership makes most sense to you?

Management vs. leadership

What people study on an MBA are the tools, techniques and
theories for analysing, planning and controlling. The task
is for an organisation to perform effectively and efficiently
and meet or exceed its goals. This feels solid; it sounds like

management. At the same time, MBAs are told that they are also in preparation for leadership in times of change and uncertainty, where flexibility, creativity and 'out-of-the-box' thinking are important. This feels less concrete. Leadership is much harder to grasp because it concerns things that do not yet exist. Both management and leadership deal with values as well as value, both address purpose as well as process, and each can claim it aims for achievement as well as attainment. Both happen in the present moment.

My take on this is that the crucial difference comes from leadership being about a future state. Management struggles with the future and acts to minimise unpredictability.

Leadership is found in many parts of life, which is one of the reasons it is difficult to define. In business, the scope of leadership is anything and everything that is a challenge to the stability or future of the organisation. Managers who are leaders are also still managers. Unless you own the company, your management task is first and foremost to protect the interests of the owners, founders or shareholders. A tension comes because leadership is a kind of exploration and this involves risk. Leaders have to be risk takers, of course, but there are limits because the new course must still perform the managerial goal of creating value.

ACTIVITIES FOR REFLECTIVE PRACTICE

1. Talk to some of your colleagues. Do they consider themselves to be managers or leaders? The more people you can talk to, the better equipped you will be to form your own definition.

2. What is the main leadership task in your organisation? How is this currently measured?

The development of models of leadership

Earlier in the chapter I told you there were four major perspectives on leadership. There are also many models and theories. In the next section I'd like to give you an example of the range available. It's not a complete list, of course, but all are well established and as you read, you might want to reflect on each from your own experience, or from examples of leadership you are familiar with.

Leadership as authority, hierarchy and innate quality

Trait theory says leaders are leaders because they possess a set of innate qualities and characteristics. 'Leaders' are born with these traits: they cannot be developed. This theory dates back to Thomas Carlyle's 'Great Man' theory in the mid-1800s. History, it was said, was the story of the biography of great men (women were almost entirely excluded). This now seems dated, but echoes of trait theory live on in the growing interest in charismatic leadership and in tests such as the 'Big Five' personality questionnaire, which assumes innate qualities play a part in our ability to undertake leadership roles. These modern traits are less to do with physical attributes than with innate psychological preferences.

> trait theory says leaders are leaders because they possess a set of innate qualities and characteristics

Trait theory relied on a **deduction** based on **inductive** observation; it saw successful examples and then drew wider generalisations and predictions based on those. For example, transactional models of leadership, where leadership is based on hierarchical positions of power over subordinates, rely on this logic. Over time, the theories and models have been adjusted, but this view of leadership can become a self-fulfilling concept.

Leadership as learned competencies

If Drucker is the first voice in management writing, veteran scholar Warren Bennis can claim the same for leadership studies. In 1985, with Burt Nanus, he published *Leaders*, which has set the tone for the subject ever since.[1] Bennis was influenced by the hardships of the Great Depression but also by the series of iconic leaders in the decades following. This formative experience comes across in his four requirements for leadership:

1 An adaptive capacity for being resilient, creative and aware of opportunities.

2 A capacity to engage followers and align them around a common goal.

3 The undertaking of a life-long process of self-awareness.

4 A moral compass or set of principles and convictions.

On top of the subject-specific knowledge each sector or business requires, Bennis is a firm believer that leadership has a moral shape and that it can be learned.

Leadership style is all about behaviours rather than personal characteristics. Leadership is what leaders are able to do and how the leader copes with the balance between concern for the task and concern for people. This model is very popular because it fits easily into existing ideas about the role of management and so is used extensively in organisations. The two sets of concerns translates nicely onto a leadership grid with five styles, developed in the 1960s by Robert Blake and Jane Mouton and shown in Figure 10.1.

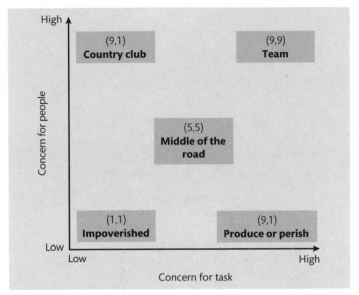

FIGURE 10.1 Leadership grid
Source: Adapted from Blake, R. and Mouton, J. (1985) *The Managerial Grid III: The key to leadership excellence*, Gulf Publishing Co. Reproduced with permission.

The grid began life describing managerial work, so its claim to say something about leadership leaves open the question whether there is any difference between the two.

Action-centred leadership theory is a straightforward framework developed by John Adair. Its simplicity makes it applicable to leadership in any of the functional areas we have covered in management, but especially to strategy. There are three parts to the model: team, task and individual (see Figure 10.2).

The skill of the leader is in balancing their attention among all three things in order to achieve targets while building morale among teams and productivity among individuals. There is an elegant simplicity to the model, which I like, but again it applies to management just as easily as to leadership.

FIGURE 10.2 Adair's action-centred leadership
Source: Adapted from Adair, J.E. (1973) *Action-Centred Leadership*, McGraw-Hill Education. Reproduced with permission.

Leadership as activities, tasks and practices

The idea of leadership as a process and not a list of attributes, skills or traits moves the topic closer to a more contextual (and strategic) view. A process suggests that leadership occupies the space between leaders and followers. Leadership can then be more distributed and may appear at many levels. The leader's role is still multifaceted but is more subtle than earlier models because followers are now just as important to the concept of leadership.

Situational leadership starts from the idea that different situations call for different kinds of leadership. It is an extension of the leadership style model because it says that a leader adapts their style and develops their skills in order to meet the varied needs in each situation. Situational leadership begins to recognise that leaders interact with followers (in fact, there is no leader until there is at least one follower). Based on the work of Paul Hersey and Ken Blanchard, the model puts forward the idea of a connection between the leader and the readiness of the follower that establishes leadership as relational.

> a leader adapts their style and develops their skills in order to meet the varied needs in each situation

There are four leadership styles, each associated with a different context in the management of people, processes and projects. The first of these is **directing** – appropriate when your followers have high commitment but low competence. This may be typical of the start of employment or kick-off of a new project; sometimes people just need to be shown or told what to do. A second, more supportive, style – **coaching** – is suitable when your followers already have some experience of what they are doing but still need or look for direction, though in this context coaching often looks a lot like training. As your staff gain in confidence, they can take more responsibility for themselves and their tasks. The third leadership style is when you remain high in terms of being **supportive** but more hands-off when it comes to you giving direction. Typically, you will intervene either when asked to, or through your own questions. Lastly, at its most developed level, situational leadership requires low levels of support and direction, and you are **delegating**, trusting that your staff will flag up any issues when they come across them. The implicit idea is that leadership is being transferred downward over time.

Situational leadership is popular in management development because it fits with conventional views of organisations as hierarchical but complex, and also with the widely held opinion that leaders should change to meet changing needs of subordinates. It relies on the leader, however, to make the running. They need to read the situation (and are therefore separate from it) and know exactly the levels of competence and commitment among those lower down in the organisation.

Leadership as humility, service and transformation

Lao Tzu, philosopher and founder of Taoism in China, managed to capture a very modern take on leadership many centuries before it emerged in our post-industrial society:

> A leader is best when people barely know he exists, not so good when people obey and acclaim him, worse when they despise him. But of a good leader who talks little when his work is done, his aim fulfilled, they will say: We did it ourselves.[2]

Several influential theories and models have said much the same.

Level 5 leadership arises from one of the most robust studies of leadership, conducted by Jim Collins, whose book *Good to Great* ought to be on every manager's reading list.[3] After a longitudinal study of nearly 1,500 companies, what Collins found surprised him. Only 11 companies made the transition from strong performance to consistent outperformance of others in their sector. In every case where this was achieved, the person in charge was not the outgoing, high-profile and larger-than-life character that usually appears as a role model in the media. Such stars may be effective in the short term, but they tend to bring division and personal ego to the organisation. Collins noted that great leaders, in commerce at least, began by surrounding themselves with the right team and then credited those people for any success. Collins also found that great leaders are strong-willed professionally while humble personally. He called these people 'Level 5' leaders. They have egos but their energy is focused in service of the organisation and not in praise for themselves (you might think back to the Erikson life cycle in Part 1 and the topic of generativity). Collins found that such leaders had often undergone a personal trauma in which they had learned this life lesson.

Good to great companies:

▌ confront current reality head-on with the belief that they
will survive

▌ take their time in getting things done – they keep steady
and do not swing wildly from one change programme or
restructuring to the next

▌ keep their business model simple – you find what is your
passion, do the one thing you are best at, engage the right
people in the process. This is sometimes known as the
'hedgehog concept', innovating only in line with what you
already do well (i.e. the hedgehog knows one thing, the fox
many)

▌ are highly disciplined in rejecting hierarchies and
bureaucracy while highly focused on promoting activity,
new ideas and entrepreneurship.

Servant leadership is an extension of the logic above. The
idea was developed by retired AT&T executive Robert
Greenleaf in the 1970s. Servant leadership is seen as part
of a participative style of management, where the manager
or leader is effective without resorting to hierarchy or
authoritative power. A servant leader, according to Larry
Spears, influences in 10 ways:[4]

▌ **Listening**: being receptive to the group and helping to
clarify what they want.

▌ **Empathy**: accepting others and seeing things through their
eyes.

▌ **Healing**: an appreciation of the natural ability of others to
be whole.

▌ **Awareness**: starting with self-awareness.

▌ **Persuasion**: building agreement through sound argument,
not coercion.

▌ **Conceptualisation**: finding and nurturing vision in self and others.

▌ **Foresight**: intuitively understanding past lessons, present realities and the likely outcome of a decision for the future.

▌ **Stewardship**: remembering to be in service of the needs of the system.

▌ **Commitment to the growth of people**: personal, professional and spiritual.

▌ **Building community**: the pursuit of societal justice, well-being and progress and concern for the underprivileged.

A servant organisation puts its people before profits. This contrasts with the conventional view of organisations as places where personal development is a nice-to-have and not a must-have. However, there is some confusion over whether servant leadership is prescriptive (this is what you should be doing) or descriptive (this is what leaders actually do). In addition, the link between the goals of the organisation and the goal of societal change is difficult to identify.

Other concepts in a similar space are authentic leadership and transformational leadership. The authentic leader is a character wished for following the wave of corporate scandals at the turn of the twenty-first century in the United States. The theory behind transformational leadership precedes this and combines the humanistic concerns with employee well-being and empowerment with some metrics around the delivery of change. The leader, in both cases, is a role model for change.

All these theories of leadership locate leadership in the role of a person who is a 'leader'. They therefore set up a contrast with the role of a person as 'manager'. It is possible, likely even, that we will always look at (or to) individuals as leaders, but the question of 'leadership' may prove to be a bit more complex than this. Can doing nothing also be an act of leadership, for example?

CASE STUDY

Three brief cases of leadership

Rosa Parks: In December 1955, civil rights activist Rosa Parks refused the driver's instruction to give up her seat in the coloured section to a white passenger on a segregated public bus in Montgomery, Alabama. Rosa had not planned this act, was not the first woman to be arrested for doing so, but her case was pursued through the US court system and became an early symbol of civil disobedience and defiance that achieved national importance and inspired others to non-violent direct action. After her death in 2005 Rosa became the first woman to lie in state in the Capitol building in Washington.

Ginni Rometty: For 100 years, IBM resolutely placed men at the head of the organisation, but in October 2011 the company selected insider Ginni Rometty to take over from Sam Palmisano as CEO and then also as Chairman (sic) a year later. She is frequently listed in global lists of powerful and influential business leaders (fewer than 5 per cent of Fortune ▶

500 CEOs are women[5]) and is credited with driving through a strategy at IBM that focuses on consulting services and development of computers with the ability to learn.

Malala Yousafzai: Malala Yousafzai had already been an activist, blogger and social campaigner for the education of girls in her native Swat valley, a region of north-western Pakistan, for two years when, aged 15, she was targeted on her school bus and shot multiple times by a Taliban gunman. One bullet went through her forehead. She survived and underwent medical treatment in Pakistan and in the UK, recovering to continue to write, broadcast and travel (while maintaining her studies) all over the world. Her demeanour and courage have inspired many and in 2012 a UN petition calling for the right of every child in Pakistan to be educated used the slogan 'I am Malala' to make its point. Malala herself spoke at the UN in 2013 and the movement continues to grow.

Where is the study of leadership going next? In Chapter 9 I looked at the way that globalising forces are affecting the size and scope of organisations, and there is an obvious connection between this and the readiness and resilience of managers to take on these international leader roles, as well as the readiness of the organisations they work for to rise to new challenges.

Leadership as a systemic phenomenon

A systems view challenges all the assumptions underpinning the last 60 years of theory in leadership development. Every organisation functions as a system. This system has a boundary, but this is not closed. In fact, the organisation knows it exists only because of those relationships with what lies outside the boundary. Open systems are unpredictable and complex and therefore you cannot hope to understand your organisation simply by analysis of its parts. This is true of leadership as well.

> you cannot hope to understand your organisation simply by analysis of its parts

Figure 10.3 shows the main contrasts between the analytical and the systems approaches.

Systemic leadership explains how a leader is only one part of the sense making of a wider context. Of course, the concept of leader is real in a social sense – someone will take or be given the role, so this view doesn't wish to do away with the idea.

Complexity theory says that an organisation is not a closed system with fixed variables and linear processes but rather

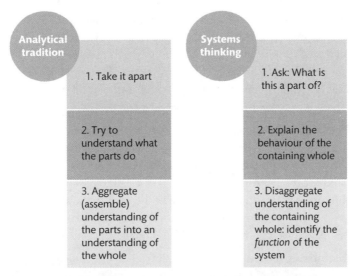

FIGURE 10.3 The contrast between analytical and systemic explanation

it is a complex adaptive system (CAS). A CAS is an open system, with too many variables at too many levels to map using conventional analysis. It also means you cannot reduce leadership to the level of an individual. Complexity leadership does, however, provide a model to reflect a concept of leadership as an emergent property distributed in the interactions between the inside and the outside of an organisation. What is also new here is that it includes the random or chance as part of leadership (every open system is subjected to the random). Under the right conditions, says this view, leadership is bound to emerge. Researchers Benyamin Lichtenstein and Donde Plowman identified four conditions for this:[6]

1. **A dis-equilibrium state**: something happens that is out of the ordinary and this initiates a real imbalance in the system. This sort of crisis is sometimes known as 'the edge of chaos'.

2. **Amplifying actions**: when a system is not in equilibrium, small actions or events can create differences that jump across in a non-linear way and produce unexpected changes in other parts. These are 'positive feedback loops' (positive here means an injection of energy into the system). If enough of these occur, a threshold of change will eventually be crossed by the system.

3. **Self-organisation**: under these changing conditions, the system will either collapse or it will reorganise itself into a new order or new state. The system is, in some way, 'learning'. The process of change here is highly creative (i.e. it is volatile and disruptive), but so eventually negative feedback loops (negative means it is self-sustaining) are needed to balance the positive ones.

4. **Stabilising feedback**: positive feedback cycles in a system will eventually be dampened by negative ones to some kind of stabilisation. These negative loops are

imposed from a higher-level system (e.g. the market). The organisation adjusts to the new situation.

In each phase leaders may choose their own actions and behaviours, which are part of the system, too. A leader may embrace and even exaggerate uncertainty when faced with it and they may act to support people in the organisation as they try to make sense of change. The leader may even act to calm things down when the system is ready to return to a steady state. The main difference between complexity leadership and other theories of leadership is that explanation of what happens is found in the way that a system works, not in the way a personality is measured. In fact, complexity leadership is not a recipe of what to do.

ACTIVITIES FOR REFLECTIVE PRACTICE

Take a look at this short TED talk by Derek Sivers entitled 'How to build a movement': www.ted.com/playlists/how_leaders_inspire. Do you agree with his conclusion? Does it change your thinking?

Leading change

One name dominates the subject of change as it intersects with conventional ideas of leadership: John Kotter. Leadership isn't about dreams and visions, it's about dealing with the fact, says Kotter, that at least 70 per cent of change projects don't work. In his research among the relatively small numbers that do, he identified a pattern for success in eight steps, shown in Figure 10.4.[7]

The inclusion of several commonly accepted features of leadership such as tenacity and vision is no surprise, but Kotter has stressed the first step ('a sense of urgency') as being the most important to leadership of change. He cautions that at each step there may be pitfalls –

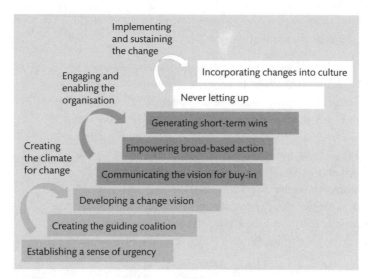

FIGURE 10.4 Kotter's eight steps of change
Source: **http://www.kotterinternational.com/our-principles/
changesteps/changesteps**, Kotter International. Reproduced with
permission.

complacency or false urgency at the start are unproductive, a
failure to build a team or an alliance to overcome resistance
to change (people tend to be very conservative when faced
with the idea of change) is another, while organisational
politics or lack of a clear vision can disrupt a reorganisation
or change project. Perhaps the most striking aspect of this
(and other change models) is its linear design.

> people tend to be very conservative
> when faced with the idea of change

A systems view, meanwhile, warns us to expect change to
be more fluid, turbulent and full of feedback loops (as well
as unintended consequences). Some of these aspects appear
only later, after the change agent (leader) has moved on. In
this case, putting too much store just in the persona of a

leader to deliver will result in disappointment. This brings us back to a general theme: learning.

The organisational development (OD) movement of the last 20 years sees leadership as located throughout the system – embedded in the 'learning organisation'. The original influences for the term 'learning organisation' were the work of Donald Schön and Chris Argyris in the 1980s[8] and Peter Senge's influential book *The Fifth Discipline*.[9] These promoted a systems perspective but failed to challenge the non-systems dogma prevalent in all hierarchical or individualistic versions of leadership.

How do you reorganise and transform without destroying the very thing you want to preserve? This is a real problem faced by everyone who finds themselves drawn to a position of change leadership.

Putting it together: how heroic is leadership?

What leaders do has much in common with what managers do, though in one respect there is a big difference. Perhaps this is the only difference that matters. Management is about trying your best to avoid nasty surprises. In all but the most trivial cases of trial and error, management does not embrace the unknown. But leadership emerges whenever we do not know with absolute certainty what is going to happen next. And because we live in open systems, we really never know what's going to happen next.

No one seems to have solved the riddle of defining leadership. Like many concepts in management, its definition shifts over time and with the fashions of the age. Our recent attitude has been that if you can't find a ready-made leader, then at least you can develop one, although complexity theory offers us a chance to look at leadership in a new light. Arguably, the one thing standing between you and leadership is the word 'leadership'.

Further reading

A classic text: *The Prince* by Niccolò Machiavelli
(2003), Penguin. A treatise on
leadership, change and power written
500 years ago but with plenty to say
that is relevant to current topics.

Going deeper: *Good to Great* by Jim Collins (2001),
Random House Business. One of the
best books on leadership.

Watch this: 'What it takes to be a great leader',
a TED talk from 2013 by researcher
Roselinde Torres, who has distilled
three questions for the twenty-first
century leader: **www.ted.com/talks/
roselinde_torres_what_it_takes_to_be_a_
great_leader**

Notes

1 Bennis, W. and Nanus, B. (1986) *Leaders: Strategies for taking charge*, New
Edition, HarperBusiness.
2 Tzu, L. (1989) *The Complete Works of Lao Tzu*, Seven Star
Communications.
3 Collins, J. (2001) *Good to Great*, Random House Business.
4 Greenleaf, R. and Spears, L. (2002) *Servant Leadership: A journey into the
nature of legitimate power and greatness*, 25th Anniversary Edition, Paulist
Press International.
5 **www.catalyst.org/knowledge/women-ceos-fortune-1000**
6 Lichtenstein, B.B. and Plowman, D.A. (2009) 'The leadership of
emergence: A complex systems leadership theory of emergence at successive
organizational levels', *The Leadership Quarterly*, 20(4): 617–630.
7 Kotter, J. (2012) *Leading Change*, with a new preface by the author, Harvard
Business Review Press.
8 Argyris, C. and Schön, D. (1995) *Organizational Learning: Theory, method
and practice*, 2nd Edition, Financial Times/Prentice Hall.
9 Senge, P. (2006) *The Fifth Discipline: The art and practice of the learning
organization*, 2nd Edition, Random House Business.

QUESTIONS FOR REFLECTION

1 What is your calling? What are you passionate about?

2 What groups or communities are you a member of? How are these activities connected to your identity as a manager?

11

Corporate reputation, social responsibility and sustainability

*Those are my principles, and if you don't like them …
well, I have others.*

Groucho Marx

In a nutshell

Business has many challenges, though few more important
than the pressing social and environmental questions facing
us today. This chapter covers three inter-related topics that
are emerging as vital for organisations if they are to endure
over time:

▌ **Corporate reputation**: starting with a clear strategy,
reputation is about consistent performance ('the show
must go on') and identity with purpose.

▌ **Corporate social responsibility (CSR)**: flowing also from
purpose, CSR is not just about acting in a moral and
responsible way, it is also about contributing to social
progress.

▌ **Sustainability**: flowing from responsibility, sustainability
deals with perpetuity, or long-term survival. Managers
used to be taught that this meant sustaining profit growth.
Nowadays it represents a wish to leave the world in a
better state than it was found.

In this chapter you will:

▌ evaluate reputation in the eyes of key stakeholders

▌ define and critique corporate responsibility in management

▌ ask how organisations should act to manage sustainably

Corporate reputation

Reputation is the extent to which an organisation remains consistent over time in the eyes of its stakeholders. A well-accepted definition of corporate reputation comes from US academic Charles Fombrun, who says it is:

> a perceptual representation of a company's past actions and future prospects that describe the firm's overall appeal to all of its key constituents when compared with other leading rivals.[1]

This is broader than brand management. We usually think of this comparison, says Fombrun, in terms of character, emotions, trust and values. The 'substance' or structure of an organisation can and will change; people come and go, products travel through life cycles of growth and decline, and assets accumulate and diminish in value, but reputation is not found in any of these things. Every subject mentioned in *The Every Day MBA* is involved with reputation.

The reason organisations pay attention to this is simple: there is a correlation between the positive regard perceived by your stakeholders and their willingness to engage in supportive activity with you. In other words, reputation impacts value creation. The risk to an organisation from reputational failure is considered as serious as any other sort of crisis.

Stakeholder management

Consistency of image really emerges through stories, so the management of reputation involves good communication and listening skills. Managers must identify important stakeholder groups or representatives to do this (a stakeholder is any interested person or entity that potentially has something to lose). In large organisations this communication process may be quite formal and can produce enough data to test perceptions widely among other non-core audiences. If you've been on a company website and seen a pop-up message asking for feedback and opinion, you've witnessed that organisation's understanding of at least one element of its reputation. In most cases, reputation management begins with two stakeholder groups: employees (who perceive the organisation's 'identity') and consumers (who perceive its 'image'). If this is as far as it gets, then you might find out to your cost that other stakeholder groups matter, too, so we need a way to widen the focus.

> the management of reputation involves good communication and listening skills

A typology of the important attributes of stakeholders was provided by Ronald Mitchell in 1997 (see Figure 11.1).

The first step is a judgement of what type of influence a stakeholder might have. In other words, how could it influence your business (positively or negatively) that any given stakeholder:

can choose to do what they want, despite you	*Power*
has a legal or contractual claim with you	*Legitimacy*
demands immediate attention from you	*Urgency*

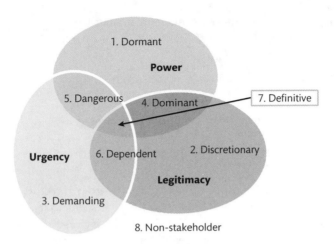

FIGURE 11.1 Mitchell's stakeholder typology
Source: Mitchell, R., Agle, B. and Wood, D. (1997) 'Toward a theory of
stakeholder identification and salience: Defining the principle of who and
what really counts', The Academy of Management Review, 22(4): 853–886.
Reproduced with permission of The Academy of Management.

When these overlap, eight possible categories of stakeholder
follow, each with its own action required:

▌ **Dormant**: groups which could impose their will but lack
the right and the need to do so. *Action: keep informed.*

▌ **Discretionary**: groups with a legitimate claim but no
power to influence anything and no pressing need. *Action:
Involve only when necessary.*

▌ **Demanding**: those that have an immediate need but neither
power nor legitimacy to enforce it. *Action: prioritise other
groups first.*

▌ **Dominant**: have both power and legitimate claims on what
you do. *Action: Keep well informed.*

▌ **Dangerous**: have power and urgency but no right or
legitimate say. They expect a say and may resort to
disruptive measures to get it. *Action: monitor and keep
engaged.*

▌ **Dependent**: lack power but have urgent and legitimate claims. *Action: manage thoughtfully as they can realign with other stakeholder types.*

▌ **Definitive**: possess all three aspects. *Action: full communication.*

▌ **Non-stakeholders**: possess no influence over you.

ACTIVITIES FOR REFLECTIVE PRACTICE

Look at this list of possible stakeholders: board of directors, management, financers, brokers, shareholders, financial regulators, industry regulators, government or government agencies, consultants, employees, contractors, customers, industry organisations, universities and schools, trade unions, non-profit organisations/charities, the media (you may add others).

Identify at least two of the key stakeholder groups for your organisation. Conduct an analysis using the Mitchell typology above.

Trust

Trust is an interesting aspect of corporate reputation. We all know what trust is – until, that is, we are asked to define it. As an idea, trust is found in every human culture. It may be identified in different ways in different places, and prized in some business models while not prized in others. But when an organisation doesn't meet the expectations of one of its key stakeholder groups, this qualifies as a risk to reputation. Trust and risk are closely related concepts. Both speculate into the future from the present, both are influenced by perceptions of the past and both involve the management of expectations.

Trust is your willingness to accept the risk that a relationship that you are involved in could go wrong. When a manager looks at this, they should do so in terms of a stakeholder's perception of the person or organisation. The questions to ask are:

▊ **Ability**: can they?

▊ **Intention**: do they want to?

▊ **Integrity**: do they hold similar values to give us a platform for resolving any disputes?

Trust is the lubricant for cooperation and economic progress.

In an ideal world, either managers would always get this right or at most there would be a gentle process of public relations, and corporate reputation would not be an issue. In reality, organisations need to manage very carefully recovery from any damage to reputation when something goes wrong. As noted in Chapter 6, with the reach and speed of social media, sophisticated consumer/special interest groups and tighter financial margins for competitive advantage, reputations can be very vulnerable. Here are two quick examples:

▊ In January 2012 McDonald's issued a tweet on its Twitter feed with the hashtag *#McDStories*. It was a modest campaign designed to highlight the hard-working McDonald's supply chain. But the hashtag was picked up by other Twitter users and within half an hour the company had received thousands of negative postings by consumers sharing their bad experience or negative feelings towards the fast-food giant. To make matters worse, all tweets with *#McDStories* automatically appeared in a feed on the McDonald's website, making the event a news story in its own right.[2]

▊ The Washington Redskins is a well-known football team in the United States and a business valued by Forbes at $1.7 billion in 2013. Following a lawsuit brought by

the Me-Wuk, a Native American tribe, in June 2014 the
US Patent and Trademark Office cancelled trademark
protections for the Redskins team name, ruling that the
term is 'disparaging of Native Americans'. The tribe
want the team's owner, Pro Football, Inc., to change the
name. The ruling allows the company to continue to use
the name but effectively removes any barrier to others
producing branded merchandise as well. Those bringing
the case were clear that they objected on ethical grounds
to the name, but despite public pressure, the owner of
the team, Dan Snyder, has refused to consider a change,
vowing to appeal.[3]

Measuring reputation

Corporate reputation is not a fixed asset, although many
companies have tried to offer a balance sheet valuation of
the premium associated with their company reputation. Nor
is it always possible to measure the effect of what are usually
said to be its main components – credibility, reliability
and trustworthiness – on the profit and loss account.
Nevertheless, the lure of analysis in management is strong
and various devices and models for reputation measurement
exist. Metrics that you might encounter for reporting
reputation include:

- opinion polls and market research
- customer satisfaction indices (e.g. net promoter score)
- financial ratios
- internal surveys and statistics (e.g. customer complaints, staff turnover)
- social media reports (e.g. aggregator sites, referrals, hits, tweets, etc.)
- regulatory compliance and quality certification (e.g. ISO).

Unlike other aspects of management, reputation is not (yet) a department or a function. Who owns reputation in an organisation, and what role it plays in decision making at each level, as well as what moral obligations in management there are, remain very difficult issues to resolve. When it comes to aligning not just to legislation but to social well-being and ethical standards, the closest topic appears to be corporate governance.

> unlike other aspects of management, reputation is not (yet) a department or a function

Governance (Chapter 8) has been defined as 'the system by which companies are directed and controlled'.[4] The scope of our definition of governance in the future will need to include the interests of more stakeholders than just the investors/owners and employees. To do this is to explore socially responsible investment in line with corporate social responsibility.

Corporate social responsibility

A corporate reputation can be judged good or bad in terms of its effects on profitability. Whether a reputation is ethical, however, requires another concept: CSR. As a manager this will bring you into contact once more with values and beliefs, which we met in a personal context in Chapter 2.

Reputation has made a business case for itself, but what about CSR? Let's starts with an influential economist and see what Milton Friedman had to say on this subject:

> There is one and only one social responsibility of business – to use its resources and engage in activities designed to increase its profits so long as it stays within the rules of the game, which is to say, engages in open and free competition without deception or fraud.[5]

Friedman rejects the idea that an organisation has a moral purpose beyond the interests of the individuals who own it. A manager's only duty, he seems to say, is to pursue profit, presumably in the belief that they can then use their wealth to better society generally. Whoever wants to put a case for CSR must therefore have an answer to Friedman's bold statement. Where Friedman saw no justification for anything beyond the healthy creation of profit, others have concluded that a definition of CSR cannot be restricted to profit maximisation. There are two reasons why CSR could be a requirement:

1 If every person has a moral duty to act in an ethical way, then so does every organisation (because an organisation is an individual in the eyes of the law). The problem with this is that managers are supposed to represent shareholder interests, so when does corporate responsibility override fiduciary duty? Do managers have the authority to think or act on wider social problems without knowing whether this is what the shareholders would do?

2 Alternatively, if an organisation exists only because it is a part of a bigger, wider system that creates a social imperative to act in an ethical manner, then managers have a moral duty to put this interest first.

The problem, according to Henry Mintzberg, is that managers are not equipped to act with CSR principles in mind.[6] Managers are promoted to senior positions on the basis of their proven ability as experts in creating value, not on their understanding of wider social issues. The fear is that if corporations are driven to seek only competitive advantage, they are more likely in their actions to create social problems than solve them.

Perhaps the greatest barrier to CSR is the difference between what people at the top say they believe and what they actually require the people in the middle to do. If these are not the same, and especially if middle management performance is tied to short-term financial goals, then any statement of CSR will look to the outside world like 'greenwash'. What's more, it can sometimes take real courage and vision in a senior manager to intervene in the 'business-as-usual' mentality to apply principles that will not necessarily contribute to the traditional bottom line.

Definitions vary, but generally it is agreed that CSR:

▌ is seen as voluntary and goes 'above and beyond' the legal minimum

▌ is balanced between multiple and wide-ranging stakeholders, not just shareholders and customers

▌ internalises external impacts. CSR brings in-house the effects and costs of corporate activity that might otherwise be met by the community (e.g. the results of waste products on the environment)

▌ is about much more than corporate philanthropy. The conventional image for CSR (see Carroll's pyramid in Figure 11.2) has been one of organisations donating funds to or promoting charitable projects, not making social progress a part of every internal business function.

Most for-profit organisations would go along with these points. Where it becomes contentious is in the next point, namely that CSR:

▌ does not put social responsibilities above economic ones. Companies always need a business case for CSR, but this case is framed by social responsibility.

This economic principle underpins the others. It may also, of course, undermine them. You can see this tension in Figure 11.2. US academic Archie Carroll identified four elements of corporate responsibility and placed them in a hierarchy.

FIGURE 11.2 Carroll's hierarchy of CSR aims
Source: Adapted from Carroll, A.B. (1991) 'The pyramid of corporate social responsibility: Toward the moral management of organizational stakeholders', *Business Horizons*, 34(4): 39–48. Reproduced with permission of Elsevier.

According to Carroll, ethical (performing in a manner consistent with societal norms) and philanthropic (sponsorship of charitable and civil society causes) responsibilities are levels that can be addressed sequentially only after lower ones have been satisfied. The phrase corporate social performance (CSP) better captures the traditional relationship between these levels, the first two of which are covered by Friedman's approach, but overall this model seems to face some problems as a hierarchy because CSR demands that all of these things need to happen simultaneously, not as a sequence.

Responsible leadership

All strategic decisions have social as well as economic consequences. Strategic decisions of big companies tend to have a bigger impact on reputation (which is measured in performance) and so larger organisations now often devote much more time and energy to CSR. Take a look at the short case about Intel's activities.

> strategic decisions of big companies
> tend to have a bigger impact on
> reputation

CASE STUDY

Intel and conflict minerals

In January 2014, US computer chip maker Intel became one of the first US companies to complete an audit of its supply chain to achieve the 'conflict-free' sourcing of tin, tungsten, tantalum and gold from the Democratic Republic of Congo (DRC) and neighbouring countries. The task took four years and the report was filed in May 2014, just ahead of a legal deadline set by the Securities and Exchange Commission (SEC).

In a white paper, Intel said:

> From the time we became aware of the potential for conflict minerals from the DRC to enter our supply chain, we have responded with a sense of urgency and resolve. We have approached this issue in the same manner as we address other significant business challenges at Intel. We first collected as much information about the situation as we could, not relying solely on our own knowledge, but also seeking insight and experience from other stakeholders and organizations with expertise in this area. We communicated with our suppliers and expressed our sense of urgency on this issue and our expectations. We met with industry peers and governmental officials, and traveled hundreds of thousands of miles around the globe to visit numerous smelters and refiners in our relentless pursuit of a conflict free supply chain.

The move to force companies to act faced legal challenges from the US Chamber of Commerce, the Business Roundtable and the National Association of Manufacturers.

Source: **http://www.intel.co.uk/content/dam/doc/policy/policy-conflict-minerals.pdf.** Reproduced with permission of Intel Corporation.

Measuring CSR

In 1994 John Elkington published a landmark book, *Cannibals with Forks*, kicking off a worldwide movement to quantify the aims of the United Nations in promoting sustainable development.[7] Elkington introduced the term triple bottom line (3BL) to illustrate his point. The bottom line has long been a euphemism for the financial performance of an organisation and a metaphor for the success or not of a business. That financial aspect is covered in Elkington's model by 'profit', to which 'people' and 'planet' are new additions (see Figure 11.3).

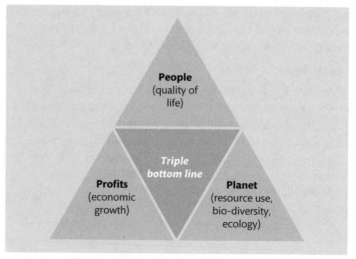

FIGURE 11.3 Elkington's 3BL

The relationship between people and profit needs to be equitable, while between people and planet it needs to be bearable, and between profits and planet it must be viable. Where these three meet, says the theory, is called 'sustainable'. 3BL has become a template for measuring CSR efforts in many organisations, but it is not the only one. Others you may come across are:

▌ carbon footprint

▌ environmental and social quality certification

▌ community relations

▌ number of suppliers/distributors/contractors who have met standards

▌ reduction of energy consumption and recycling.

Around the world there are new and exciting examples of people and organisations working to a business agenda subtly different from the established shareholder value model. Here are just a few examples:

▌ Social partnerships are inter-organisational and enable NGOs, not-for-profits and businesses to work together on societal or environmental collaboration.

▌ Cooperatives and Fairtrade Foundation initiatives (in 2012 sales of Fairtrade products in the UK reached £1.5 billion and the mark enjoys a 78 per cent consumer recognition).[8]

▌ Open source projects such as Wikipedia and Linux, and modern versions of barter economics offer alternative views to free market capitalism.

ACTIVITIES FOR REFLECTIVE PRACTICE

Does your organisation have a statement or a position on CSR? If so, have you looked at it? Try to identify the assumptions used in its construction. If not, would this be a good exercise for your organisation?

Sustainability

Sustainability is a hot topic in business and is set to become even hotter over the next 10–30 years. The globalised business model we know in the developed and developing world is built on a presupposition of growth and unrestrained access to natural resources, which our technology is designed to continue to find new ways to exploit. This is a deep-rooted cultural attitude, informed by scientific methods and political ideals that have incrementally provided wealth creation and social change for 200 years. But it wasn't until 1987 that the UN World Commission on Environment and Development defined sustainability as:

> development that meets the needs of present generations without compromising the ability of future generations to meet their needs.[9]

sustainability is a hot topic in business and is set to become even hotter

There are three sorts of inter-linked change, driving an interest in sustainability at the macroeconomic level:

- **Demographic:** changes in size and form of the world's population, including divisions based on relative levels of equality and poverty (1.2 billion people live in extreme poverty). These changes include an ageing population, falling rates of child mortality, falling birth rate and a peak in world population of about 9 billion by 2050.

- **Ecosystems:** these have always exhibited variations over time in biodiversity and resource availability but are under extreme pressure in the next 50 years. The world's agriculture has become big business, putting pressure on land use, access to fresh water, reduction of forests, pollution of the oceans and seas, and resulting in an overall dramatic reduction in biodiversity.

▌ **Climate**: again, the planet has also seen patterns of change over time, but our use of fossil fuels and other accelerants is producing enormous amounts of evidence of positive feedback loops that are contributing to global warming.

Sustainable development is political, economic and social. It encompasses resource planning and strategy just as much as values, mission and vision statements. In the same vein, because of the suggestion that current business practices may be directly contributing to the three types of crises above, a new type of leadership or management thinking – perhaps a whole new way of understanding business – may be required. Here are three of these challenges:

▌ **Sustainable consumption**: managing supply and demand to ensure basic needs are met and quality of life maintained while minimising the use of natural, non-renewable resources and controlling emissions of waste and pollutants.

▌ **Sustainable production**: management of the supply chain within ecological limits to maintain biodiversity and regeneration and – ethically – avoid the exploitation of populations or people.

▌ **Sustainable development**: in systems thinking, no system can be understood except in terms of the larger system of which it is a part. Sustainable development has proven difficult to define because our ability accurately to predict the future has been so poor.

The goal of true sustainability is threatened by rapid changes in land cover (more deserts, fewer forests) and land use, the exploitation of natural resources beyond their capacity for regeneration or replacement, pollution and the effects of climate change.

Best Foot Forward (UK)

It is often said that you can't manage what you can't measure. This was very much the belief in the world of environmental management in the early 1990s when Oxford-based Nicky Chambers, founder of Best Foot Forward (BFF), was working with business to improve environmental performance. Sustainability was a niche intellectual concept with little practical application.

When the idea of an 'ecological footprint' was invented, it seemed an excellent way to measure and communicate the concept of sustainability to novice audiences. BFF was set up in 1997 with the clear mission to apply the footprint methodology to three scales – individuals, communities and organisations. The business went on to become one of the best-known sustainability consultancies in Europe, with blue-chip clients such as Coca-Cola, PepsiCo, Tesco and IHG.

As Nicky says: 'The idea of a resource-constrained world is now mainstream. The challenge is to design a new economy and new business models to respond to a changed agenda. The new economy and the businesses therein must create shared value within the means of nature; to improve quality of life for the human race without degrading the natural resources which are the ultimate source of our wealth and well-being.'

Reflecting a move from building awareness to helping clients make the transition, BFF was acquired in 2013 by Anthesis, a global, full-service, specialist sustainability consultancy. It is no longer enough to be a socially responsible business. 'We are approaching an era of "business with a purpose", where business is part of the solution to huge challenges we face – by improving quality of life as well as protecting the natural resources on which we rely,' says Nicky.

Source: Quotes supplied by Nicky Chambers, June 2014, email correspondence. Reproduced with permission.

The Base of the Pyramid

The Base of the Pyramid refers to the approximately 3–4 billion people in the world who live at an economic level significantly lower than the 1 billion people who live in the 'mature' countries, where needs and wants are largely met. It was first put forward by two economic strategists, C.K. Prahalad and Stuart Hart.[10] This is the 'survival economy' – where meeting basic daily needs is a struggle and where billions of people live on just a few dollars a day. Yet the Base is also a massive business opportunity, full of local vigour, innovation and entrepreneurial promise. There is potential, too, for an entirely new economic model based on alternatives or variants of capitalism.

Sitting between the Base and the peak is an aspiring middle class of at least 2 billion people whose needs are now being met, but whose wants will inevitably put further pressure on a delicate ecosystem. The middle of the pyramid attracts the majority of the FDI and other investment by MNEs and is likely to continue to be an extension of existing technology.

ACTIVITIES FOR REFLECTIVE PRACTICE

Visit TED.com and watch the Hans Rosling talk entitled 'The magic washing machine': **http://on.ted.com/Washing**.[11] This is one of several engaging TED talks Rosling has given. How would you describe his worldview? How does it compare with yours?

The Base is largely still ignored by MNEs, except in philanthropic gestures. Any organisation with a business model addressing this segment is synonymous with the pyramid Base itself. 'Mature world' business models will not work at the Base, so the poor are not just another source of consumer demand to meet in the same way that we have described in earlier chapters. The market is for goods or services that are sustainable at that level. Without question, the keys to economic emancipation at the Base include elements such as education and control of the reproductive process by women, as these are the only proven routes for a population out of poverty. Economic activity that promotes sustainable livelihoods is long-term and holistic socially responsible investment, and needs to work respectfully with the vitality and innovation often driving the desire for a better life.

Putting it together: critical thinking now equals integrated thinking

Reputation pushes at us from the past, sustainability pulls us in from the future. Still, our responsibility for action sits here in the present. Sustainable used to mean how an organisation or industry could continue to grow at an acceptable rate (with an acceptable rate of return) into the future. Since the Second World War, decades of economic, corporate and management energy have gone into promoting the rights of individuals, firms and national economies to be a little bit selfish and to take larger slices of the pie. As long as the pie could grow, this approach worked.

This is about to change. The world is showing undeniable signs of ecological wear and tear, the mature economies will continue to age and the effects of our technologically advanced lifestyles may also contain some serious unintended consequences. All informed agencies now agree: this is no longer a question for the long term. Reputation has always mattered, but it may now rest on an organisation's sense of being part of a wider web of connections and inter-related systems.

Perhaps this alternative form of governance will need stewardship rather than leadership. This means swapping individualistic behaviours for collectivist ones. It does not reject the idea of wealth creation or technological progress, but it does change the parameters of how value is measured by organisations.

Further reading

A classic text: *The Ecology of Commerce: A declaration of sustainability* by Paul Hawken (2010), Harper Paperbacks. One of the more influential books to have emerged from the sustainability movement.

Going deeper: *The Oxford Handbook of Corporate Reputation*, editors Michael Barnett and Timothy Pollock (2014), Oxford University Press.

Watch this: 'The business logic of sustainability', CEO Ray Anderson delivers a must-watch talk at TED in 2009: **www. ted.com/talks/ray_anderson_on_the_ business_logic_of_sustainability**

Notes

1 Fombrun, C.J. (1996) *Reputation: Realizing value from the corporate image*, Harvard Business School Press.

2 **www.telegraph.co.uk/technology/twitter/9034883/McDonalds-McDStories-Twitter-campaign-backfires.html**

3 Shannon Bond, 'Redskins' trademark protections cancelled', 18 June 2014, FT.com.

4 Cadbury Committee, 1992.

5 Milton Friedman, 'The social responsibility of business is to increase its profits', *The New York Times Magazine*, 13 September 1970. © The New York Times Company.

6 Mintzberg, H. (1983) 'The case for corporate social responsibility', *Journal of Business Strategy*, 4(2): 3–15.

7 Elkington, J. (1999) *Cannibals with Forks: Triple bottom line of 21st century business*, Capstone.

8 **www.fairtrade.org.uk/en/media-centre/news/august-2014/ businesses-back-fairtrades-autumn-campaign**

9 World Commission on Environment and Development (1987) *Our Common Future*, Oxford University Press.

10 Prahalad, C.K. (2007) *The Fortune at the Bottom of the Pyramid: Eradicating poverty through profits*, Wharton School Publishing.

11 Rosling is a Swedish statistician and population expert with a very engaging presentation style.

QUESTIONS FOR REFLECTION

1 Construct a stakeholder map of your career position. Who has an interest in or an expectation of you? Where should you put your time and energy?

2 Revisit the management roles discussed in Chapter 1. Do you see any to which you need to pay special attention in the future?

12
Reflective practice: management stripped bare

I don't make predictions, and I never will.

Paul Gascoigne

In a nutshell

Business pundits think management academics overcomplicate the world. Academics think pundits oversimplify it. This leaves you, the practitioner, stuck in the middle, needing to get on with your job but also aware that there are limits to your abilities and knowledge. How do you make sense of it all?

In *The Every Day MBA* my aim has been to present an informed and selective overview of the content and thinking you would find at a business school and to suggest that applying those concepts also involves an evolution in your own thinking. You have been given practical prompts to apply in your management practice along the way. A lot of these have suggested you talk to and share with others, and this is very important. You've also been challenged to think about your work in a more reflective way and I hope you have attempted to apply this curiosity to your daily job. As you seek your competitive advantage in your career, an enquiring mind could be the most important qualification on your CV. This final chapter contains several ideas that look beyond the book.

In this final chapter you will:

▌ take business back to its minimum elements

▌ find six ideas to boost your management thinking for the future

▌ be invited to explore action learning

Management: the empty space

In 1968 British theatre director Peter Brook wrote a short book about acting, called *The Empty Space.* Here is an extract:

> I can take any empty space and call it a bare stage. A man walks across this empty space whilst someone is watching him, and this is all that is needed for an act of theatre to be engaged. Yet when we talk about theatre this is not quite what we mean. Red curtains, spotlights, blank verse, laughter, darkness, these are all confusedly superimposed in a messy image covered by one all-purpose word.[1]

Brook's intention was to strip away all the thinking about our concept of 'theatre' in order to find its essential, minimum components – an empty space, an actor and an audience. That's it. According to Brook nothing should be added unless it adds to the situation. Be wary, he says, of the temptation to add ornament without getting the basics right.

Is thinking this way useful to your management practice? Yes, it's vital. Management is a noisy topic and if you want to understand it you need to strip it of its ornaments and pretensions. When you get down to those basics, I think you'll find three things:

1 **A need:** the 'empty space' of business. The unmet need is a positive space, full of potential, but it must be i) conceivable (it can be met and without losing money) and ii) morally acceptable (in that society).

2 **A consumer**: a consumer is implied by the need and by a provider.

3 **A provider**: a provider is also implied by the need and by a consumer.

Over the years, we have added many layers to these basics (the MBA is guilty of ornament, too) but at heart management is the deliberate and purposeful orchestration of these inter-relationships. There are many skills you will develop in your career. In the jobs you hold, choosing among conflicting options for ideas, resources and actions takes knowledge and experience. You'll need honesty, a strong work ethic, flexibility and mental agility and a lot of other things, that's true, but without a doubt the skill that will bring you mastery is self-awareness.

> you'll need honesty, a strong work ethic, flexibility and mental agility

The Every Day MBA is a start. If you have read this book in anticipation of future study, or a move further into management, then notice which chapters or ideas caught your attention – and dig deeper yourself. If you have read this to refresh your thinking after graduating with your own MBA, then hook back into the excitement (not the stress) from your course – and continue your journey.

Self-awareness requires curiosity, but I would like to add a thought to this. In your curiosity, acknowledge, without judgement, things as they are. Why is this important? First, this stance is a core component of mindfulness, an interesting and ever more popular subject in adult learning. Second, we all have a tendency to filter what we see through thinking biases. Here are just three:

▌ **Confabulation**: the tendency to fill in the gaps when recalling the past. We like to make a coherent story so when we can't remember the details of what happened, we make them up.

▌ **Hindsight bias**: the way we convince ourselves, after the event, that we knew things were going to happen that way all along. To do this, we carefully select information that now supports our 'clairvoyance'.

▌ **Confirmation bias**: the big one. Managers suffer from this all the time. Even you. Confirmation bias is when we settle on a position, solution, opinion or answer and then start to look for data that support our view. The cure for confirmation bias is to start your enquiry from the position of 'I don't know ... let's find out'.

You need a way of standing back from what you are observing in order to be fully aware of it. So, as you read the next section, why not practise the art of noticing your thought and reactions, without judging.

Six key lessons for your management future

I offer the ideas below to support your further development. Each is a statement and also an activity for reflective practice. The first three relate to managerial activity and the last three are intended for your wider personal development.

1 You won't learn how to manage an organisation in a classroom

In management, the right way to grow is by applying practice to theory. But first you need the practice. There is no substitute for being in the workplace if you want to learn the ropes in management. There are many managers who have done an MBA in their mid to late 20s who suspect that if they had waited another 5 or 10 years, they would have got a lot more out of it. They're right. Organisations are the collective efforts of human beings – a frustrating, complicated, complex and wonderful resource – and learning how to manage them is a contact sport. Master the basics, get the experience and earn your stripes first.

The classroom can, however, be a great place to learn something about yourself. If you can combine the self-reflection of learning with others to the application of method and theory to your management experience (especially your management mistakes) you may see some dramatic results in your career. Of course, even without access to the business school classroom, you can still find many ways to learn (see the final section in this chapter for an example of a method for this).

2 Know how value is defined in your organisation

Value has been a recurring theme in *The Every Day MBA*. The importance of value creation is one of the few things that all management experts agree on. The trouble is that there are so many ways to define and measure it. In a publically traded company such as Apple, for instance, value is undoubtedly measured by the economic return on investment for stockholders. In health service provision, by contrast, value may be the achievement of target improvements in public health. In a family firm, it could be ensuring the next generation has a livelihood.

We tend to monetise it, but value looks different wherever you go. If you don't know how it is defined where you work, find out. If no one in your organisation knows, then either you're working in the wrong company or there is a fantastic opportunity for you to lead a transformation.

3 Know what your business is worth

Not everything should be summed up in financial terms but
valuation is important. It does not require that you know
finance inside out; you just need to know enough at least to
start to answer the question of the worth of your business.
Why? There are lots of reasons. You may be part of an
acquisition process, or it may become critical in litigation,
but most commonly it gives you more power for business
planning and negotiating external sources of funding. If you
don't know what the business you are in is worth, find out.

Remember, when it comes to what things are worth, time is
the measure of all things. American investor Warren Buffett,
whose company Berkshire Hathaway is ranked by *Fortune*
as the 18th largest in the world and consistently outperforms
the market (and who famously suggested that while price
is what you pay, value is what you get), is a firm believer
in the unexciting but critical skill of business valuation.
Equally, you may also want to bear in mind that worth and
value are not necessarily the same thing. Einstein put it this
way:

> Everything that can be counted does not necessarily count;
> everything that counts cannot necessarily be counted.

> when it comes to what things are worth,
> time is the measure of all things

4 There is no limit to learning

You can never be 'full' of knowledge and it is impossible
to run out of things to learn. This is because the nature of
knowledge is not cumulative. For many, the truth of 'the
more I know, the more there is to know' first comes as a bit
of a shock, but it is then quite liberating. Think about what

this means to you in your management practice and career and then consider the following.

Learning thrives on sharing

Sharing is always a better business strategy than not sharing. For example:

▌ Sir Tim Berners-Lee, inventor of the World Wide Web, has never wavered from the ideal, famously tweeted by him live at the opening ceremony of the London Olympics in 2012, that 'this is for everybody'.

▌ Elon Musk, an extremely successful investor in IT and new technologies, is also head of Tesla motors, a company making electric vehicles. Tesla is acknowledged as having patented a superior new battery design, but in June 2014 the company announced that it would share all its technology patents.[2] This may be the move that kick-starts real change among the world's automotive companies, which have lagged behind in developing a switch to non-hydrocarbon means of transport.

▌ The decision by the founders of TED to place hundreds of videos online started a revolution in open-access sharing of knowledge.

You can learn a lot about your managerial identity in a classroom

This is the biggest opportunity for personal development open to you as you get older and as you become more experienced. All you need is to be curious, awake and rigorous in your thinking. This may require a real change in you. If you do an MBA, make sure you find the right course, with the right cohort. In that case, a business school education can really make all the difference. If you only have the workplace, make sure you are speaking and learning from those around you who have more experience.

5 Your future career is not written in your past

I think this is huge. Most of us don't realise it, though. We like to hold on to a sense of where we have come from – it's an important part of maintaining an identity – but a lot of us sleepwalk our way through life never realising that we only actually ever live it in the present.

Carl Jung said that the purpose of the second half of our lives is to understand the first. I don't start the MBA Personal Development module at Henley with career goals. Rather, we begin with a guided exploration of students' life stories. This is not because they should use the past to determine the future. Quite the contrary – I do it so that they can eventually be free from the control that their past has over them. From there we can really start to explore liberating goals.

6 In the end, what matters is working things out for yourself

My final lesson is the hope that you will eventually be able to see and work things out as they actually are for yourself. If you want total freedom to act, this can only come from within you, not from a doctrine. When you start work, the structure and purpose of business and management are given to you. Freedom in management comes when you no longer need validation of your conclusion by others. When you accept without question the tools, methods and even theories of others in your work, you are taking for granted whatever they took for granted.

> freedom in management comes when you no longer need validation of your conclusion by others

You are unlikely to find this out during an MBA, or just from reading a book. The final part of an MBA usually includes a piece of management research or a larger strategy project. It is often where a few things fall into place, including a much stronger sense of self-confidence and critical thinking skills. Even without that, if you can find more flow and happiness at work, if you can build resilience and develop a passion for what you do, and if you can understand something of the wider social context of being a manager, then you will have succeeded in starting a very worthwhile journey.

Putting it together: management is learned from others but defined by you

Every manager should know how to start an investigation of an organisational problem and how to generate evidence on which to propose solutions and make decisions. This is profoundly important because it moves from applying management tools in order to fix problems to self-awareness about your view of the world and how to define what a problem is. *The Every Day MBA* finishes with an introduction to another method you can use to combine knowledge with experience: action learning (AL). The central idea in AL is, as British academic Reg Revans says:

> There is no learning without action and no (sober and deliberate) action without learning.[3]

AL is an educational approach to solving complex problems. It was developed by Revans in the decades after the Second World War and has since been used in many leadership and productivity initiatives. The formula for AL is:

$$L = P + Q$$

where L is learning, P is programmed knowledge and Q is insightful questioning.

AL involves regular group discussions but the key is to put individual follow-through into action. AL requires a small set of people from diverse backgrounds who contract to cooperate over a period of about 18 months. It is also a good method to trigger reflection.

An action learning set is the small group tackling important organisational problems. Membership must be voluntary and each person needs to have an apparently intractable problem that requires action. The requirements for action learning are:

▎ an issue or problem

▎ turn-taking, good questions, fresh ideas

▎ time to reflect on experience

▎ no hierarchy, no power games

▎ confidentiality

▎ action.

You may already be part of such a group at work but it is called something else (especially if you are part of a quality improvement initiative). One of the best ways, if you can, of engaging in the strength of AL is to be part of a set where none of the members works for the same organisation or in the same industry. Action learning groups can be facilitated or they can run themselves. This doesn't matter. What does matter is that an attitude of curiosity, respect and learning becomes part of the development of skills and behaviours that solve real management issues.

I wish you every success in your career and in your journey of self-awareness as a manager.

Further reading

A classic text: *The Reflective Practitioner: How professionals think in action* by Donald Schön (2010), Ashgate. A classic from 1983 that has influenced many other thinkers while resisting all temptation to turn itself into another two-by-two matrix or questionnaire.

Going deeper: *Action Learning for Managers* by Mike Pedler (2008), Gower Publishing. A short and easy-to-digest introduction to AL.

Finding Your Element: How to discover your talents and passions and transform your life by Ken Robinson (2014), Penguin Books. Robinson's own 'element' is communicating his passion for learning. It's infectious.

Watch this: 'Trial, error and the God complex', a TED talk from 2011 by economist Tim Harford that asks us to choose a new mindset for our problems and puzzles: **www.ted.com/talks/tim_harford**

Notes

1 Brook, P. (2008) *The Empty Space*, Penguin Modern Classics.
2 Foy, H., 'Tesla lifts bonnet on its electric car tech secrets', *The Financial Times*, 13 June 2014.
3 Revans, R. (1982) *The Origins and Growth of Action Learning*, Chartwell-Bratt.

QUESTIONS FOR REFLECTION

1 Go back and look at your responses to the six activities in the introduction to Part 1. How has your perspective changed? Are there ways that you have changed your perspective? How are you better informed about your work or yourself?

2 Where do you go from here? What's your next step?

What did you think of this book?

We're really keen to hear from you about this book, so that we can make our publishing even better.

Please log on to the following website and leave us your feedback.

It will only take a few minutes and your thoughts are invaluable to us.

www.pearsoned.co.uk/bookfeedback

Glossary

Selected terms used in MBA thinking

Subject-specific glossaries can be found quite easily from the reading that you can do after *The Every Day MBA*. This list is more personal. Some of the entries have been used in this book while others are simply terms about learning that I believe every manager should know.

Abduction Great scientists start with a hunch, or an informed guess, to build the idea behind a theory. Abduction is the name of the form of inference they use for this. Abduction means looking at the world around you and applying a rule or pattern from somewhere else to explain the data you have. For example, 'seed is to plant as egg is to bird' is a very simple form of abductive inference.

Assumption A frame of reference; a short cut and basis for belief that is accepted by us and unnecessary to examine before we act. However, to learn, grow and change we must challenge our assumptions and examine those things we take for granted (see **Reflection**).

Behaviourism A branch and theory of psychology that is interested in observable, measurable actions rather than thoughts or mental constructs. Originally it was made popular in management by the work of John Watson and B.F. Skinner in the 1930s. Because management is seen as a matter of what managers do, this approach lives on in modified form (e.g. in the study of organisational behaviour).

Best practice   A current, structured and repeatable process that has proven successful (i.e. with a positive impact in terms of value). Best practice is always aligned to existing processes and systems and strategic intent. Over time, best practice is evaluated by others and can become a benchmark that other organisations can copy or adopt.

Business model   Every organisation has a business model because every organisation is a collection of purposes, methods, norms, strategies, relationships and activities that keep it going. By default, whatever your organisation actually does – that is its business model. There is no shortage of academics, consultants and pundits to suggest new business models, however.

Bloom's taxonomy   Benjamin Bloom first developed a hierarchy of objectives in education in the 1950s, with the aim of encouraging educators to take into account cognition, emotion and action.[1] The taxonomy has been very influential, despite some criticism. It consists, in order, of 'remember', 'understand', 'apply', 'analyse', 'create' and at the top 'evaluate'. To understand why our education system is set up the way it is, also read John Dewey.

Coaching (executive)   It is fashionable now to expect managers to coach their subordinates. This is dangerous. A coaching mindset may be powerful, but power can cause conflict of interest or, worse, it can corrupt. The essence of coaching is to be of use to another person as they identify and work towards goals – on their terms, not yours. Coaching needs positive intent, genuine curiosity and insightful questions, as well as action.

Competency   Competencies are behaviours that you are judged to do well, or should do well. This has become the most popular way of thinking about what management is. Job descriptions are designed around the competencies that the post holder should exhibit, and performance appraisals usually measure results against a prescribed list of behaviours. The problem is that in different contexts different behaviours can prove highly destructive.

Deduction Deduction is a form of inference. It is widely used in theory building to form hypotheses to test (i.e. falsify) a theory. Deduction starts with a premise, which is a general statement of a covering rule, and moves to a specific case (a hypothesis). If the covering rule is correct, any conclusion deduced must logically follow (e.g. if A = B and B = C, then A = C). If the conclusion is false, then the premise must be incorrect and a better covering rule needs to be determined.

Emotional intelligence (EI) Of interest to many, including occupational psychologists, EI has been popularised in the books of Daniel Goleman[2] but draws on the earlier work of Howard Gardner ('multiple intelligences').[3] EI is the attempt to measure how adept you are at monitoring yours and others' emotional states and to use this ability to guide behaviours. There is no general agreement as to whether these are learnable skills or innate traits, or both. Or neither.

Flow An idea developed by Hungarian–American psychologist Mihaly Csikszentmihalyi to describe the mindset or state of being fully involved and engaged with what one is doing.[4] At work, flow is experienced when the level of challenge faced and level of skill available are both sufficiently advanced. It is often linked to moments or periods of high productivity by individuals or groups.

Game theory A mathematical technique developed by John von Neumann to calculate the outcomes of conflicting situations among theoretical players of a game, all of whom are assumed to be rational and in possession of full information.[5] It has been applied to economics and to operational and strategic decision making but is a poor indicator of management decisions in open, social systems.

GMAT   The Graduate Management Admissions Test is a widely used device for helping to secure a place on an MBA programme. GMAT tests for a candidate's analytical, quantitative and verbal reasoning skills. However, it does not test management experience or acumen and there is no correlation between a high GMAT and good management decisions.

Heuristic   A heuristic is a way of working to a solution to a problem through the use of an approximate series of trial and error. Heuristic thinking is intended to be fast and uses short cuts, rules of thumb or educated guesses. However, if the underlying structure is not reflected in the rule of thumb, it can lead to serious error.

Human relations movement (HRM)   The HRM grew as a contrast to the scientific movement (see **Technical rationality**) and is an interdisciplinary approach to maximising productivity that draws on social psychology and sociology. HRM has become synonymous with the idea of employee engagement and empowerment as essential to motivation, but does not challenge the hierarchical status quo.

Induction   Induction is a form of inference. Moving from the particular (observed) to the general (unobserved) only from observation of a set of examples in the past is inductive thinking (e.g. inductively, the next number in the sequence 2,4,6,8 ... would be ... 10, but there is no way of working this out logically). The conclusion of an induction is always wider than its set of premises. It is often the basis for heuristic (i.e. rule of thumb) thinking.

Information   Given how often managers go on about it, it is surprising how rarely the word information is defined in business. The common-sense definition might be 'data', but there are many types of data that do not become information. Information is news (to you) of a change or difference. Only data that make a difference become information.

Knowledge management   The practical activity of capturing, storing and using information and data within an organisation and also the managerial activity of using this to create value. There are various interpretations of what this means, but they broadly divide between a focus on data storage and a focus on communicational exchange. Personal knowledge management (PKM) is the use of social media to coordinate the storage and transfer of your knowledge.

Lineal (vs. circular) causation   A lineal relationship is one where a series of causes and effects in a sequence does not end back where it started. Lineal sequences can occur in closed systems. The opposite of lineal is recursive, which is the circular causality of feedback loops found in complex systems. Linear is a mathematical term for a relation between variables that can be plotted in a straight line. The opposite of linear is non-linear.

Mentoring   The process whereby a person with experience offers guidance and encouragement to someone younger or more junior. Mentors are expected to give advice and share their experience. Mentoring requires time, effort, trust and confidentiality on both sides and should be for a fixed duration. Mentoring is not coaching.

NLP   NLP (Neuro-linguistic Programming) was started in the 1970s as an attempt by Richard Bandler and John Grinder to codify the effective patterns used by therapists and counsellors in treating various psychological situations. NLP suggests that anyone can overcome cognitive obstacles by modelling certain techniques. It has grown in popularity but remains controversial in its claims.

Paradigm (shift)   An over-used term in business and management, it was the subject of an influential book by Thomas Kuhn in 1962.[6] In science, a paradigm is the orthodox framework of ideas that members of a community can no longer legitimately dispute. These become, over time, the worldview. But science learns, and when there is a change in what we all agree we know at a fundamental level, Kuhn calls this a paradigm shift.

Pareto principle   The 80/20 rule, and perhaps the most elegantly simple management principle in circulation. The heuristic that 80 per cent of one thing is often attributable to 20 per cent of another (e.g. when 80 per cent of your turnover comes from 20 per cent of your customers). Knowing this can help you direct your efforts to where they will have greatest impact.

Profit maximisation   The idea that it is a manager's duty to maximise short-term profits that seems to drive much decision making. This view is sometimes challenged and there are many counter-examples, but in practice it still dominates much economic theory as well as popular conceptions of businesses and the people who run them.

Reductionism (vs. holism)   Western science prizes intellectual activity that seeks the simplest, most economical explanation. This, however, may not be the only way of explaining the world around us and in fact may be counter-productive when taken to extremes. The counter-argument is that explanation may also come from seeing one context in terms of a larger whole.

Reflection   This definition is a good starting point: 'Reflection is a process, both individual and collaborative, involving experience and uncertainty. It is comprised of identifying questions and key elements of a matter that has emerged as significant, then taking one's thoughts into dialogue with oneself and with others.'[7]

Seminal   Any work, opinion or publication that strongly influenced others or appears transformed in later developments may be described as seminal, or formative. Seminal works are those that you should go back to in order to understand and decode those later works, which may have taken ideas as given (see **Assumption**).

Technical rationality   The view that management consists of the solving of practical problems through the application of scientific theory and method. Specialist technical knowledge is what sets the manager apart from the non-manager, a view championed in the period between the two world wars, and though things have changed, many organisations still value a rigorous, systematic and standardised application of professional knowledge.

TED   In 1984 a multi-disciplinary conference on Technology, Education and Design in Monterey, California kicked off a worldwide phenomenon. In 2006 online access to hundreds of TED talks opened the world to a new source of information. The TED format allows experts to make engaging presentations of up to 18 minutes in length (no selling allowed) to invited audiences drawn from many disciplines.

Web 2.0   In terms of content, the first manifestation of the World Wide Web was 'one to many' communication. Web 1.0 grew as a new marketplace or channel for buying products (the 'shopping cart' web). The next phase, which we call Web 2.0, is many-to-many communication. Content is created by and freely shared among users on social media platforms. Web 3.0 is said to be 'the internet of things', using mass data created, shared and used by various devices in our environment.

Notes

1 Bloom, B.S.. Engelhart, M.D., Furst, E.J., Hill, W.H. and Krathwohl, D.R. (1956) *Taxonomy of Educational Objectives: The classification of educational goals. Handbook I: Cognitive domain*, David McKay Company.

2 Goleman, D. (1996) *Emotional Intelligence: Why it can matter more than IQ*, Bloomsbury Publishing.

3 Gardner, H. (2006) *Multiple Intelligences: New horizons in theory and practice*, 2nd Edition, Basic Books.

4 Csikszentmihalyi, M. (2002) *Flow: The psychology of happiness: the classic work on how to achieve happiness*, Rider.

5 von Neumann, J. and Morgenstern, O. (2007) *Theory of Games and Economic Behavior*, 60th Anniversary Commemorative Edition, Princeton University Press.

6 Kuhn, T. (2012) *The Structure of Scientific Revolutions*, 50th Anniversary Edition, University of Chicago Press.

7 Jay, J.K. and Johnson K.L. (2002) 'Capturing complexity: A typology of reflective practice for teacher education', *Teaching and Teacher Education*, 18(1): 73–85.

Index

Do you want your people to be the very best at what they do?
Talk to us about how we can help.

As the world's leading learning company, we know a lot about what your people need in order to be better at what they do.

Whatever subject or skills you've got in mind (from presenting or persuasion to coaching or communication skills), and at whatever level (from new-starters through to top executives) we can help you deliver tried-and-tested, essential learning straight to your workforce – whatever they need, whenever they need it and wherever they are.

Talk to us today about how we can:

- Complement and support your existing learning and development programmes
- Enhance and augment your people's learning experience
- Match your needs to the best of our content
- Customise, brand and change it to make a better fit
- Deliver cost-effective, great value learning content that's proven to work.

Contact us today:
corporate.enquiries@pearson.com